G000128549

Advent/Christmas Resources For Young And Old

A Christmas Anthology

Mary Lu Warstler
Lynda Pujadó
J. B. Quisenberry
May Dembowski
Suzanne E. Fisher
Arlys M. Winkler

CSS Publishing Company, Inc., Lima, Ohio

ADVENT/CHRISTMAS RESOURCES FOR YOUNG AND OLD

Some scripture quotations are from the *New Revised Standard Version of the Bible*, copyright 1989 by the Division of Christian Education of the National Council of the Churches of Christ in the USA. Used by permission.

Some scripture quotations are from the *Revised Standard Version of the Bible,* copyrighted 1946, 1952 ©, 1971, 1973, by the Division of Christian Education of the National Council of the Churches of Christ in the USA. Used by permission.

Some scripture quotations are from the *Holy Bible, New International Version.* Copyright © 1973, 1978, 1984 International Bible Society. Used by permission of Zondervan Bible Publishers. All rights reserved.

Some scripture quotations are from the *King James Version of the Bible,* in the public domain.

Library of Congress Cataloging-in-Publication Data

Advent/Christmas worship resources for young and old : a Christmas anthology / Mary Lu Warstler ... [et al.].
    p.   cm.
  ISBN 0-7880-0840-4 (pbk.)
  1. Christmas. 2. Worship programs. 3. Advent. I. Warstler, Mary Lu.
BV45.A38   1996
242'.33—dc20   96-12417
                                        CIP

This book is available in the following formats, listed by ISBN:
    0-7880-0840-4   Book
    0-7880-0841-2   IBM 3 1/2
    0-7880-0842-0   Mac

PRINTED IN U.S.A.

Table Of Contents

1

Let's Have A Fruitful Christmas Season

An Original Skit
By May Dembowski

Running Time

Twenty-five minutes (including one two-minute break)

What's It About?

This is a skit written for a Christian Women's Pre-Christmas-Season program, suitable for a ladies' breakfast, brunch, luncheon, and so forth. It is not evangelistic, but rather an idea-filled dialogue which gives some practical suggestions for keeping Christ in Christmas and heading off the usual frenzy of the busy season.

How Many Characters?

The four characters are women who are meeting for their regular kaffee klatsch and discussing the hectic holiday season coming upon them.

How Involved Is The Production?

The actual production of the skit can be as sophisticated or as simplistic as is practical for those putting it on. Since the characters are seated at a table, they could get away with having scripts in front of them, saving having to memorize all lines. Props are simple household things.

Whether on a stage with professional lighting and sound amplification or set up on the same level as the audience, the scene should be small and intimate; props should be kept in close with nothing to draw the eye away from the group at the table.

Spoken lines do not require a lot of acting or projecting, especially if the personalities of the players match the skit's characters. There's room for spontaneity and improvisation for the sake of personalizing or customizing the message.

Surprise, Folksy Options!

If this skit is played for a group of women in a small church or community, the names of the characters may be changed to the actual names of the women in the cast. Care should be taken to match the characters' descriptions when casting.

There are six topics discussed in the skit. Each time conversation changes direction there is a natural hesitation (brief break). During any of these breaks, it may be appropriate to invite guests (audience) to refill their coffee cups and pass the "goodies" around. In fact, this would be preferable over allowing such activity to cause distractions during dialogue. The women in the skit might also enact this. The program emcee would then call the assembly back to order and the skit would proceed.

The Scene

Jane's kitchen, afternoon kaffee klatsch time

Props

Kitchen dining table with four chairs (positioned around back and sides of the table); two extra chairs off to the side for coats, Carol's and Marcy's handbags or tote bags (each containing writing pad and pen[cil]); notebook and pen(cil) for JANE, which is beside her on the table or on a smaller table nearby; coffee pot containing brown liquid preferred by cast (cold tea, real coffee); four coffee mugs, spoons, creamer and sugar bowl or reasonable facsimile. A tray of "goodies" may be on a smaller table nearby to serve during optional breaks.

Costumes

Everyday casual clothes in season. JANE might wear an apron if it seems in character. Choice of dress may help create an atmosphere (hectic Christmas season) if women look somewhat harried — hair done up in rollers, sweatshirts with rolled-up sleeves and jeans, and so forth.

Special Options

If the occasion for putting on the skit is a festive pre-Christmas function, bright holiday winter wear would be called for. Extra props such as gift-wrapped packages stacked on a chair, a lighted Christmas tree and boxes of decorations, Christmas tablecloth on the table, or bright red mugs would help set the scene.

Cast Of Characters

JANE: The hostess (age 40-55), quiet countenance but not mousey, probably the spiritual leader.

CAROL: A housewife and mother (thirtyish), frank and sometimes outspoken and/or witty.

MARCY: A young mother (age 25-30), eager for ideas and wisdom for raising her children.

MAY: A maternal figure (fifties or so) with lots to say, exuberant.

Let's Have A Fruitful Christmas Season

Scene Opens

JANE, CAROL, and MARCY are seated at Jane's table. Carol's and Marcy's coats are on the side chair. One leaves her handbag on the chair, while one keeps her handbag by her feet. JANE is pouring coffee and CAROL and MARCY are helping themselves to "fixin's" and chattering happily about how good it is to be together, weather, whatever ... all talking at once.

MAY enters noisily, throwing her coat and handbag off onto side chair, obviously late, hurrying, and breathless.

(Women at table immediately focus on MAY.*)*

JANE: Goodness, May, what have you been up to? You look like you're going to collapse. Here, have some coffee. *(Pours coffee and pushes mug toward* MAY.*)*

CAROL: *(Sliding sugar and creamer toward* MAY*)* Yeah, sit down and take a load off your feet.

MAY: *(Taking coffee and saying "thanks," then fixing it)* Well, that time is here. Every year it gets here sooner, and I have to admit, I'm getting to dislike the whole thing!

(ALL continue to sip coffee naturally throughout conversation.*)*

MARCY: What whole thing? You mean Christmas?

MAY: Yes, I mean Christmas!

JANE: Shame on you. How can you say that about Christmas?

MAY: Oh, it's not that I really don't like Christmas. After all, I know why we celebrate and that's what I long to do ...

CAROL: *(Interrupting)* Honor the Lord, you mean. I know what you're talking about. Every year, I determine to put Jesus back into my hectic holiday, but ...

MAY: *(Interrupting)* Every year it gets more hectic!

JANE: I remember when my Christmases were ALWAYS like that.

CAROL: WERE?! What happened? Did you die and go to heaven?

JANE: No, it's just that they're so much better now. I can honestly say I enjoy the whole season and even begin thinking about it months ahead.

MARCY: Well, that's probably your whole secret right there — thinking ahead.

MAY: It's all so discouraging. That's one more thing I determine to do … plan ahead. But I end up not doing it.

JANE: Well, I have to say that since I started planning ahead, even right after Christmas for the next year, I …

MARCY: *(Interrupting)* Whoa! That's really early! How do you plan THAT far ahead?

JANE: First of all, by taking a few minutes after the holidays to evaluate. In fact, last year I made a notebook so I wouldn't forget what the Lord showed me.

MARCY: A notebook? Planning in January? Sounds good, but I'm not sure it would work for me.

MAY: Well, one thing for sure, nothing works without the Lord's grace. And I'll be first to admit that I don't ask for His peace and wisdom as I should.

JANE: That's it right there, May. We need to be more like Jesus. The Fruit of His Spirit: love, joy, peace, patience, gentleness, goodness, and faith … have got to be shining through all the way.

MARCY: Well, amen to that! Now where does a notebook come in, Jane?

JANE: *(Reaching for her notebook and showing it while she talks)* See here? I divided a page into two columns. On one side, I wrote all the bugaboos that robbed my family of Christmas joy. Then I asked the Lord for wisdom. In the other column I jotted down ways to prevent or cope with each problem. And I've already begun to take action to head these things off. Started in October, in fact.

CAROL: Sounds like a great idea. Every year, the same insanities wreck the joy of our Christmas and I always wonder why I didn't see them coming.

JANE: Probably some unexpected things will sneak up that I'll have to deal with. But with my prevention notebook and God's help, I really do expect my home to be more peaceful this year.

(MARCY fusses about getting pencil and notepaper from her purse to start taking notes. Others follow her example. JANE warms their coffee.)

This is an appropriate place to take a short break.

MARCY: Okay, Jane. So I get a notebook. Now what do I put in it about Uncle Charlie? Everybody's got an Uncle Charlie!

JANE: You mean the one who monopolizes every conversation at the big family party? Loud? Coarse? Argumentative?

CAROL: *(Interrupting)* A boor and a pain in the neck! Yeah, I've got an Aunt Del like that.

MAY: *(Laughing)* I'll bet they come early and stay late, too.

(ALL groan and carry on at once about this.)

CAROL: I used to dread seeing Aunt Del coming.

MARCY: Whaddya mean, "used to"?

MAY: I know. You moved and didn't give her your new address, right?

JANE: You prayed her into a condominium in Florida?

MARCY: I know. She died and went to heaven.

CAROL: None of the above, girls. I put her to work.

MARCY: Somehow, I don't find that too exciting. Putting Uncle Charlie to work? He's in the way as it is.

JANE: Let her explain, Marcy. There's gotta be a way to handle the Uncle Charlies with the patience and kindness that Jesus would have exhibited. Maybe Carol's found a solution.

CAROL: Well, what I really mean is that I appealed to Aunt Del's better nature. I prayed about it and the Lord showed me a few things.

MAY: *(Cynically)* "Better nature," she says.

JANE: *(Gently elbowing* MAY*)* Shhhhhhh!

CAROL: Well, Aunt Del's hyper and overbearing ... because she's so excited and glad to be with everyone!

MARCY: So's Uncle Charlie. But he gets so obnoxious, he ends up fighting with half the family or taunting the kids 'til they cry.

(ALL agree and murmur to each other about the problem.)

CAROL: They aren't dummies, you know. They hear the snide remarks behind their backs and feel the rejection when people leave the room.

MAY: Okay, so what was that better nature? What did you do?

CAROL: First I asked the Lord to shine through me and help me greet Aunt Del with a loving look rather than a hurried, impatient scowl. A gracious countenance can make a big difference … brings out the best in people.

JANE: Agreed! And what else?

CAROL: I had already made a list of last minute things to do — taking coats to the bedroom, filling water glasses, whipping the cream. I kept the list out of sight, but handy for me. And I just asked her to help.

MARCY: Didn't she resent being put to work?

CAROL: Not a bit. As a matter of fact, it made her feel needed, wanted, loved, useful. As usual, she stayed after all the others had left, so I asked her to help clean up. It so happens Aunt Del loves to be in the kitchen, and I zeroed in on that. I suppose you would have to ask the Lord to give you wisdom for finding your Uncle Charlie's niche, Marcy.

MARCY: Uncle Charlie always wants to give everybody a drink, and starts mocking us as soon as he arrives because we don't have a bar to set up.

JANE: Put him in charge of the punch bowl … and the coffee pot!

MARCY: I wonder if that would work. He'd probably make fun of it all the while.

CAROL: So what?! When he realizes you really need him to take over the responsibilities of serving all the coffee, punch … whatever … he might get too busy to act so foolish. It's worth a try anyway.

JANE: Even if he's silly or obnoxious this year, he may actually look forward to it next year. Maybe your love and patience will bring out the best in him. Like she said *(glancing toward* CAROL*)* it's worth a try.

MAY: Something like that even worked well with my husband and kids when we had a houseful of company. Whenever I remembered to take them aside, explain my plans and give them specific responsibilities, they became helpful instead of awkward and underfoot.

(Two women at one end of the table talk excitedly to each other in low tones. The other two are making notes in animated fashion.)

This is an appropriate place to take a short break.

JANE: I feel sorry for the kids at this time of year. They get so excited, and mothers are screaming. I marvel that they come away with any good memories at all.

MAY: I finally figured out how to make memorable and happy times for my kids. For one thing, I marked the dates right on the calendar for cookie-baking and such and counted these as real appointments … letting nothing get in the way.

MARCY: I just can't imagine having fun making cookies with a bunch of kids. Cleaning up the mess is hardly worth it. I don't have enough patience, I guess. Kids botch it so. Crooked cutouts, horrible colors, flour all over …

MAY: Maybe you don't control it enough.

MARCY: What does THAT mean?

MAY: I mean, they don't have to put awful colors together. You can put out the colors you want them to use.

JANE: But wouldn't that take away from their own fun and expression?

MAY: Not really. Not if you give them some choices. And if you're doing it right along with them, helping, guiding, and laughing with them at their mistakes.

MARCY: But at this time of year, I'm just too busy for that kind of attention.

MAY: It's the only way to survive! I asked a kindergarten teacher how she could stand teaching all those little kids at once. She answered that since it was her main job, she didn't have to let anything else get in the way. Whatever the project, when you work with children, it's best to give them your undivided attention. Supervising, making suggestions, teaching, guiding ... AND THAT INCLUDES CLEANUP TOO ... really saves time AND your nerves in the end.

CAROL: I'll agree with that. It's so tempting to do it myself. But my mother-in-law made sense when she advised me a long time ago, "If you don't let the children do things, they can't learn."

MARCY: I guess the key is to pray, plan, schedule, and follow through ... and look for God's patience and joy.

(ALL nod to each other in agreement, make notes, sip coffee.)

This is an appropriate place to take a short break.

CAROL: I've got a challenge for you. How can we go about putting Christ in our Christmas when most of the family is anti-anything-religious?

MAY: That IS a challenge! I'm never sure what to do … so I do nothing … and feel crummy about it.

MARCY: We asked my grandfather to read the Christmas story and share a bit one year. But he got preachy, and the kids got very itchy. And giggly, in fact.

JANE: There's the hitch. Ya can't get preachy. That doesn't mean you can't read the Word or talk about the Lord, though. But you really must ask Him what to say. Jesus talked to sinners, remember, but He didn't shake his finger at them.

MAY: I know one thing. If the Lord asks me to lead a family devotional time ever again, I'll do it HIS Way.

MARCY: What do you mean?

CAROL: Did you botch it up?

MAY: Kind of. I intended to read from a catchy tract, lead some carol singing; and I even lined up a couple of the kids to sing little solos. But halfway through I backed off, thinking I was getting too heavy.

CAROL: Backed off? How?

MAY: I didn't do all I planned … cut it short. I didn't give it my best shot and watered down the message.

JANE: What happened? Didn't they like it?

MAY: Oh yeah, they liked it. They would have enjoyed more, as it turned out.

MARCY: What makes you think you failed?

MAY: Conviction.

CAROL: You mean the Lord showed you that you cut it too short?

MAY: He showed me what it could have been. I had been afraid of what people might think. The funny thing is, they all think I'm the family fanatic anyway, and they expect me to do something *(somewhat mockingly)* "religious." They like it, in fact, if I keep it informal, laugh some, read scripture from a modern translation. It makes them feel good … as if their consciences are clear for the holy season.

CAROL: In other words, you're saying, "Go for it!"

(ALL enthusiastically nod and verbally agree with the idea.)

MARCY: You know, people love to hear from little children. I could have my kids read verses, sing songs, pass out scripture promises. Even say a blessing at dinner.

JANE: Great idea! And here's something I find works, too. I explain that we are going to go around the table and everyone thank God for something. It's important to stress that everyone say JUST ONE THING. That keeps the ones who are good with words from intimidating the shy ones. Give examples … like "Thank you, Lord, for the snow today." Even if some are silly or unspiritual, it's an exercise in focusing thoughts on the goodness of the Lord.

(ALL nod to each other in agreement, make notes, sip coffee.)

This is an appropriate place to take a short break.

CAROL: Okay, I'm ready! … *(Turning to new page in notebook and poising pencil, ready to make notes)* … Who's got some new party ideas?

MARCY: Here's an idea that worked great for me last year. I love to entertain with nice serving pieces, Christmas punch bowl and all, but it means getting all that stuff out and cleaning it up …

CAROL: *(Interrupting)* Isn't it the truth! I have lovely things in my cupboard and end up using throwaways.

MAY: So what's your idea, Marcy?

MARCY: I scheduled three parties all on the same weekend … one for the neighbors, a family gathering, and one for our prayer group.

JANE: Three parties in three days?!

MARCY: Yep. Even rented some chairs over the weekend so we wouldn't have to use the piano stool, step stool, and all that nonsense.

MAY: But you must have cooked for three weeks!

MARCY: No way. Since the guest list for each party was different, I used the same menu for each, and made simple dishes in double and triple batches. And kept it all cold in my walk-in cooler … *(ALL look at her questioningly)* … the garage!

JANE: And where did you get all the necessary serving trays and such?

MARCY: Well, as I said, I already had some nice things to get out and use, and then I used my imagination … covered a ratty-looking tray with foil and a paper doily … *(ALL are making notes enthusiastically and nodding)* … baskets lined with red paper napkins … and for an elegant but EASY dessert, I made individual Jell-O®-and-pudding parfaits in clear plastic cups … and served them on paper dessert plates … with paper doilies, of course … stuff like that.

JANE: You know, even regular plates or pie plates look elegant with paper doilies on them. And here's a trick … a foil-covered magazine makes an elegant hot pad!

MAY: One time I used oil lamps on my tables for soft mood lighting. They burn longer than candles and seem safer in some ways.

(ALL are buzzing as if discussing more ideas as they write notes.)

This is an appropriate place to take a short break.

MARCY: Now, May, I'd like to hear how you make such quick, neat work of the cookie detail.

CAROL: She probably buys them.

(ALL chuckle and agree.)

JANE: That's what I do.

(ALL turning on JANE in fun, "shame on you," and so forth.)

JANE: Okay, okay. So, how do you do it, May?

MAY: Okay. No-muss, no-fuss, speedy cookie detail! I make my cutout dough a day or two ahead. Then I pick out four or five favorite cookie cutters, with simple shapes. I bake so many stars, so many wreaths, and so forth. When it's time to frost them, I use … oh, I don't know if I can say this … well, er … store-bought frosting in the can!

(ALL laughingly show mock hilarious horror, "shame, shame, boo, hiss," and so forth.)

CAROL: *(Patting MAY on the back)* Yay for May!

MAY: If possible, I use throwaway utensils. Frosting detail is like an assembly line. First, some cookies with white icing. Decorate with colorful sprinkles or sugars. Then I tint some frosting with yellow and do some more, then green and so on. The main thing is to KEEP IT SIMPLE. No experimenting. Green sugar on green icing, red sugar on pink icing. Any color on white. You can't goof up that way. They look like you've fussed for hours. Final touch? Display them with some "can't fail" fudge or foil-wrapped candies on a tray decorated with a …

ALL: *(Interrupting with raised voices)* A paper doily! *(Laughter)*

MAY: And Jane's not the only one to buy cookies. When I have a cookie-decorating party for my grandchildren, I buy animal cookies for them to decorate. They're easier to handle and quicker. They love it.

CAROL: I guess we all try to do too much.

JANE: We probably should make a list of all the things we want to do and scratch half of them off.

MAY: Probably more than half. I'm sure our families would be happier if we did less and smiled more.

MARCY: Amen to that! *(Collecting her things and getting ready to go)* Well, I gotta go, girls. *(Putting on coat)* I'm going home to catch a few minutes before the school bus arrives to make some plans. *(With emphasis)* Some PEACEFUL … SIMPLE … ENJOYABLE ones.

(CAROL and MAY also get ready to leave. JANE stands back as hostess, holding one's coat or whatever seems natural and appropriate.)

CAROL: Me, too. And I'm going to stop and pick up a notebook, too. *(Turning to JANE)* Thanks for the idea, Jane.

MAY: Well, busy times ahead, ladies. We won't meet like this until after the holidays, but I expect we'll all have some praise reports of a peaceful and joyful Christmas.

MAY, CAROL, MARCY: *(All leaving and calling individual good-byes)* Good-bye! ... Thanks, Jane, for the coffee! Merry Christmas!

JANE: *(To departing guests ... **and also to audience**)* Bless you all! Happy Holidays! And have a joyful, wonderful, FRUITFUL Christmas in the Name of Jesus!

Finale

It would be appropriate for all the cast to regroup in Jane's kitchen and sing to the audience "We Wish You A Merry Christmas!"

2

A Service Of Light

A Worship Service For Christmas Eve
By J. B. Quisenberry

Production Notes

The four biblical characters, King David, Elizabeth, the Innkeeper, and Mary, may either be played by teenagers or adults. They may be in full costume and speak from the front of the sanctuary, or they may be voices out of the darkness. While the monologues need not be memorized, the readers should be familiar enough with the lines to have eye contact with the congregation if they are presented as characters in full costume.

The sermon should be no longer than twelve minutes.

The production time is about 55 minutes.

Prelude

Call To Worship
L: Rejoice! Jesus Christ, the light of the world, has come!
P: Glory be to God!
L: Glory be to God in the Highest!

Introit   "Come Thou Long-Expected Jesus"
                                                              verse 1

The Psalter   Psalm 97
L: The Lord reigns; let the earth rejoice; let the many coastlands
be glad!
**P: Clouds and thick darkness surround the Lord; righteous-
ness and justice are the foundations of God's throne.**
L: Fire goes before the Lord, and burns up his adversaries round
about.
**P: The Lord's lightnings illumine the world; the earth sees
and trembles.**
L: The mountains melt like wax before the Lord, before the Lord
of all the earth.
**P: The heavens proclaim God's righteousness and all the
people behold God's glory.**
L: All worshipers of images are put to shame, who make their
boasts in worthless idols; all gods bow down before the Lord.
**P: Zion hears and is glad, and the daughters of Judah rejoice,
because of your judgments, O God.**
L: For you, O Lord, are most high over all the earth; you are ex-
alted far above other gods.
**P: The Lord loves those who hate evil, preserves the lives of
his faithful, and delivers them from the hand of the wicked.**
L: Light dawns for the righteous, and joy for the upright in heart.
**P: Rejoice in the Lord, O you righteous, and give thanks to
God's holy name!**

Hymn   "O Come, All Ye Faithful"
                                                          verses 1 and 3

Lighting Of The Advent Wreath

Pastor: During the last four Sundays, we have tried to prepare our hearts for the coming of the Lord. Each Sunday, we lit a new candle on our Advent wreath, and with each candle lighting, we took another step closer to this holy night. Like God's love for us, the wreath is a circle with no beginning and no end. Tonight, as we celebrate our Savior's birth, we will light the candles once again. As we light them, let us renew our personal relationship with God and with each other.

First, we will light the candle of Repentance, so that its light may burn away our sins.

David: Repentance, now that's something I know all about! When you get right down to it, it's the only thing we human beings *can* do if we're honest with ourselves. I mean, God knows us inside and out. He knows all our petty jealousies, all our weaknesses, all our sins. Oh, we may be able to hide them from the people around us. We may even be able to hide them from ourselves for a short time, but we can't hide them from God.

I tried to hide behind my crown and my royal robes. I had the power to hide my inexcusable actions from the people of Israel. I was David, the King! Even the few who knew what I had done did not dare question me, but I could not hide from the Almighty God! His light burned into my guilty soul. The amazing thing is that, as dark as my sins were, repentance opened up my soul to God's cleansing power, and he made me clean again!

With all my faults, it was from my lineage that God brought forth Jesus Christ, the Messiah!

How many of you, I wonder, are hiding sins behind masks of respectability and modern social practice? God knows all of your secrets. Open your souls up to his light. Repent, and he will make you clean.

Musical Interlude "O Come, O Come, Emmanuel"
verse 5 with no refrain

(While this may be sung by the congregation, it is more effective as either an unaccompanied vocal solo or a solo by a muted trumpet or other brass or woodwind instrument. During the music, the first candle is lit.)

Pastor: Next, we will light the candle of Obedience. It reminds us to study God's Holy Word, and to be open to his guidance.

Elizabeth: Obedience. That's a good word to describe my cousin, Mary. There was nothing worse for a woman of our time than to be pregnant and unmarried. Yet, when the Angel of the Lord came to her, she did not hesitate. She did not question. "Behold the servant of the Lord," she said. At that moment, the Son of God began to grow within her womb.

She knew as well as any woman what her pregnancy would mean. She knew the finger-pointing and the whispers of rejection she would have to endure, and yet she was obedient to God's will. Her heart was always open to his guidance.

I think that is why she was chosen to bear God's Son. Her trust in God was complete, and her obedience was absolute. In return, God gave Mary the Peace that only he can give. He was with her all the days of her life.

He can be with you, too, if you are open to his guidance and obedient to his will.

Musical Interlude   "O Come, O Come, Emmanuel"
                                                                   verse 2 with no refrain
(Muted accompaniment may be added to the soloist from the first interlude, or a second vocalist or instrumentalists may perform this piece. During the music, the second candle is lit.)

Pastor: Now we will light the third candle on our Advent wreath, the candle of Love. We have received the overwhelming love of God in the gift of his only begotten Son. This candle calls on us to love others as God first loved us.

Innkeeper: Love. That was a word I didn't use much before I met that young couple from Nazareth. Love is not profitable, you see, and profit was all that was on my mind, especially that night. Caesar's tax decree was a real windfall for me and the other innkeepers in Bethlehem! My inn was full to overflowing! Then *they* knocked on my door, a poor, working-class couple with a few small bags and a mangy donkey. I had been turning ragtags like them away all evening. I was about to do the same to them when my wife intervened.

"What about the stable?" she asked.

"Smart girl!" I thought. "We'll make some money off of these two yet!"

That was not at all what my wife had in mind, though. Her eyes were shining as she smiled at the young woman on the donkey. It was then that I noticed the woman was expecting. Women have a soft spot for those things, you know, so we showed them to the stable and I got on with my work.

Later that night, the young woman had her baby, and my wife insisted that I come out with her to see him. That's when it happened. The moment I looked into that little boy's eyes, I was filled with such warmth and such love! There aren't words to describe it! That moment changed my whole life. I see the world differently now. Why, I have even been known to *give* a room to someone who doesn't have the money to pay for it! When people come to my door, I no longer judge them on the basis of how fine their clothes are, or how much I am likely to make from them. Now people are more important to me than profit is.

No, love isn't profitable, at least not in the worldly sense; but the love I received from that baby boy has filled my whole life. I can't help but share it with others! Jesus can do the same thing for you, if you open up your hearts to him, and receive the light of his love!

Musical Interlude   "O Come, O Come, Emmanuel"
                                        verse 7 with no refrain
(This piece should be slightly less muted than the first two. Another vocalist or instrumentalist may be added. During the music, the third candle is lit.)

Pastor: Next we will light the fourth candle, the candle of Joy. This candle reminds us of the "Joy unspeakable" that Jesus offers to those who believe in him, the joy that frees us from our worldly doubts and fears.

Mary: Joy! Yes, joy is what Joseph and I felt that night, and every moment of our lives thereafter. It is a joy far beyond simple happiness or worldly pleasure. That joy grew as my Son grew within me. It was joy that banished my fears on the road to Bethlehem. It was God's joy that led us to the stable with its sweet smell of fresh cut hay and the warmth of the animals. It was joy that eased the pain of my labor, and that brought forth my dear Son, Jesus. It was joy that filled our hearts as Joseph and I marveled at those ten perfect little fingers and those ten precious little toes. It was that joy unspeakable that flowed from my Son's heart and into the hearts of the shepherds, and the wise men, and all of the others that have known him through the years. It is God's joy that has filled all of my days, and that gave me comfort in the dark hour of my Son's death. It was joy that raised him from the dead on the third day, and it is that joy indescribable that Jesus Christ offers to each one of you! Open your hearts to him! He is waiting for you. Receive his joy!

Musical Interlude   "O Come, O Come, Emmanuel"
                                             verse 6 with refrain
(For this piece, all mutes should be removed. The music should sound louder and more up-tempo. The refrain may be repeated twice, if so desired. During the music, the fourth candle is lit.)

Pastor: The time of preparation is at an end. Our Lord, Jesus Christ, is indeed Emmanuel, God with us now and forever! In celebration of his birth, we will now light the Christ candle that stands in the center of our Advent wreath. It reminds us that if Jesus is at the center of our lives, his light will shine in our hearts, and he will be with us for all eternity! Praise be to God!

Musical Interlude "O Come, O Come, Emmanuel"
verse 4 with refrain

(This last piece should be at full volume and played with great joy. The refrain may be repeated twice, if desired. During the music, the Christ candle is lit.)

Hymn "Hark! The Herald Angels Sing"
verses 1 and 3

Prayer *(In unison)*

Gracious and loving God, as we celebrate tonight the glorious birth of your Son, our Lord, Jesus Christ, we are overwhelmed by your love! We know that we are not worthy of such a gift.

We have looked into our souls and seen our guilt; but your light has made us clean. We have pledged to study your Holy Word and to be open to your guidance. Help us to fulfill that pledge. We have been filled with the light of your redeeming love. Help us to share it with others. Finally, we have been blessed with the joy indescribable that you offer to all who will call upon your name. Help the joy to flow from us to people everywhere. Make us instruments of your light, dear Lord, that it may shine throughout the earth.

We pray in the name of your dear Son, Jesus Christ, who taught us to pray …

The Lord's Prayer

Anthem

Old Testament Lesson Isaiah 9:2-7

Offering

Gospel Lesson Luke 2:1-14

Hymn "O Little Town Of Bethlehem"
verses 1 and 3

Sermon

Hymn "Silent Night"
verses 1-4

(As the organist plays through the hymn, the acolytes may take a flame from the Christ candle and offer it to the people to light candles that they hold individually. The acolytes would light the candle of the first person in every pew, and then the flame would be passed down the pew from one person to the next until all candles are lit. Then the lights would be dimmed and the hymn would be sung by candlelight. The hymn should be printed in the bulletin so that the people will not have to hold a hymnal while they hold their candles.)

Benediction

Final Hymn "Joy To The World"
verses 1 and 4

Postlude

3

A Service Of Love

A Celebration Of Christian Brotherhood For The Entire Congregation With An Old-fashioned Christmas Pageant

By J. B. Quisenberry

Production Notes

This service may be done by either a large or small number of people. It is designed to involve children of all ages as well as adults. Children three years of age and older may be used as angels and shepherds as long as there is an older child to guide them. There may be as few as three angels or a whole "heavenly host." There are traditionally at least two shepherds, but there can be many more. Some of the younger children may even be dressed as sheep to accompany the shepherds. Mary and Joseph are best played by sixth graders, as they are required to hold their places longer than the others. The readers may be junior high or high school age or adults. The King James translation of the Christmas story has been used; that is the most traditional and universal version.

The only set required is a manger set up in the front of the sanctuary. The costumes may be authentic clothing or simple bathrobes.

The anthem may be sung either by an adult or a children's choir.

The foreign language hymns may be sung by a choir, but they work best when done by a soloist or small group. High school students who are studying a foreign language generally enjoy this chance to show what they have learned. These hymns also give adults who speak another language or who are from another country an opportunity to share something very special with their church family. The bulletin should include a short English synopsis of each foreign language hymn.

This service is very versatile. It may be used as a worship service for Christmas Eve or Christmas Day by simply eliminating the pageant instructions and the last phrase of the welcome. It is also a very good service for community worship that includes several congregations of different ethnic origins.

If the sermon is no longer than ten minutes, the approximate production time is fifty minutes.

Prelude

Welcome

Welcome, and peace to you all! With the gift of his Son, God has joined all believers into one spiritual family. All over the earth, the same familiar story will be read from the same Holy Book as Christians remember our Savior's birth. In every nation, hearts will thrill to the joyous music of the season.

Music is, after all, the one true universal language. It speaks not only to our minds, but to our hearts and our souls as well.

So, as we celebrate the birth of Jesus today, we will decorate our service with the music of other lands. In this way, we will join our hearts to the hearts of our brothers and sisters in Christ all over the world. Come and remember the humble birth of our Lord, as our children reenact it in innocence and love.

Introit   "O Come, All Ye Faithful"
                                                          verse 1

Call To Worship
L: Jesus is God's gift to the whole world.
P: We come together today to remember that gift, and to share his love.
L: Let us gather in joy to worship the God of Love!

Hymn   "Hail To The Lord's Anointed"
                                                    verses 1, 2 and 4

Advent Candle Lighting

Call To Prayer
L: The Lord be with you.
P: And also with you.
L: Let us pray.

Prayer Of Confession *(In unison)*

Gracious God, you would have all of your children embrace each other in brotherly love, but all too often we let worldly

31

differences like race, language, and culture come between us. Forgive our lack of understanding and our fears. Help us to see beyond temporal concerns. Open our eyes and our hearts to your limitless love so that it might guide our words and our actions. Nationality and language are not barriers to you. Your Good News rings out clearly all over the world! Let it sing in our hearts and unite our spirits forever! Amen.

Pastoral Prayer

The Lord's Prayer

Hymn   "Away In A Manger"

Offering

Doxology

The Psalter   Psalm 98

L: O sing to the Lord a new song, for the Lord has done marvelous things! God's right hand and holy arm have gotten the victory.

P: The Lord has declared victory, and has revealed his vindication in the sight of the nations.

L: The Lord has remembered his steadfast love and faithfulness to the house of Israel.

P: All the ends of the earth have seen the victory of our God.

L: Make a joyful noise to the Lord, all the earth;

P: Break forth into joyous song and sing praises!

L: Sing praises to the Lord with the lyre, with the lyre and the sound of melody!

P: With trumpets and the sound of the horn make a joyful noise before the Ruler, the Lord!

L: Let the sea roar, and all that fills it, the world and those who dwell in it!

P: Let the floods clap their hands; let the hills sing for joy together before the Lord, who comes to judge the earth. The

Lord will judge the world with righteousness, and the peoples with equity.

Anthem   "Love Came Down At Christmas"

The Pageant

Reader 1   Luke 2:1-7
(MARY and JOSEPH enter from the back of the sanctuary and proceed to the manger set up in front.)

And it came to pass in those days, that there went out a decree from Caesar Augustus, that all the world should be taxed. And this taxing was first made when Cyrenius was governor of Syria.

And all went to be taxed, every one into his own city. And Joseph also went up from Galilee, out of the city of Nazareth, into Judea, unto the city of David, which is called Bethlehem, because he was of the house and lineage of David, to be taxed with Mary his espoused wife, being great with child.

(At this point, MARY and JOSEPH should be at the manger. JOSEPH should stand to the right of the manger, and MARY should kneel to the left of it. As the reading goes on, MARY should take the baby out from its hiding place in the manger and hold and cuddle it. She may then lay it back down in the manger if she wishes. JOSEPH should also center his attention on the baby.)

And so it was, that while they were there, the days were accomplished that she should be delivered. And she brought forth her firstborn son, and wrapped him in swaddling clothes, and laid him in a manger; because there was no room for them in the inn.

Special Music   French Hymn "Il Est Né Le Divin Enfant"
                    (or two verses of another foreign language hymn)

(During the song, the SHEPHERDS enter at the back of the sanctuary and proceed to the front. They pause at a point between the front pew and the communion rail where they pantomime watching over sheep.)

Reader 2 Luke 2:8-15

And there were in the same country shepherds abiding in the fields, keeping watch over their flocks by night.

(The FIRST ANGEL *enters from the side and proceeds to the center of the communion rail, with her back to the manger and facing the* SHEPHERDS. *Upon her arrival, the* SHEPHERDS *immediately fall to their knees and hide their faces.)*

And lo, the angel of the Lord came upon them, and the glory of the Lord shone round about them; and they were sore afraid. And the angel said unto them, Fear not: for, behold, I bring you good tidings of great joy, which shall be to all people. For unto you is born this day in the city of David a Savior, which is Christ the Lord.

(At this point, the SHEPHERDS *look up at the* ANGEL, *but remain on their knees.)*

And this shall be a sign unto you: Ye shall find the babe wrapped in swaddling clothes, lying in a manger.

(The other ANGELS *enter from the side, and stand on either side of the* FIRST ANGEL.)*

And suddenly there was with the angel a multitude of the heavenly hosts praising God, and saying, Glory to God in the highest, and on earth peace, good will toward men.

(The ANGELS *proceed to the manger, arranging themselves on either side of it and slightly behind it. The* FIRST ANGEL *should stand directly behind the manger.)*

And it came to pass, as the angels were gone away from them into heaven, the shepherds said one to another, Let us now go even unto Bethlehem, and see this thing which is come to pass, which the Lord hath made known unto us.

(The SHEPHERDS *stand during this passage and pantomime an excited conversation. At the end of the passage, they proceed to the manger and kneel before it, being careful not to block the view of the manger from the congregation.)*

Special Music   Spanish Carol "Pastores A Belen"
(or two verses of another foreign language hymn)

Reader 3   Luke 2:16-20
And they came with haste, and found Mary, and Joseph, and the babe lying in a manger. And when they had seen it, they made known abroad the saying which was told them concerning this child. And all they that heard it wondered at those things which were told them by the shepherds. But Mary kept all these things, and pondered them in her heart.

And the shepherds returned, glorifying and praising God for all the things that they had heard and seen, as it was told unto them.

Special Music   German Hymn "Still, Still, Still"
(or two verses of another foreign language hymn)

Reader 4   Conclusion
And so it happened on that night many years ago. God gave all people the gift of salvation in the form of a tiny baby humbly born in a manger. From the beginning, God's great gift was universal, offered not only to the local Judean shepherds, but also to three kings from the east.

These three kings were not at all like the people Mary and Joseph were used to. Their dress, their language, their culture, perhaps even the color of their skin must have seemed quite strange to the people of Bethlehem.

None of these things mattered to Jesus. It was their hearts that he was interested in. So, like the familiar shepherds, the three foreign kings were welcomed by the Holy Family. Like the shepherds before them, these powerful men knelt humbly in the straw before the newborn King of kings. Like the shepherds, they received the love, and the peace, and the unspeakable joy that only Christ can give.

We, too, have received the precious gift of salvation, and by receiving it we have been joined to all believers all over the world. Our Savior calls on us to look beyond the differences that separate us, and embrace with love our brothers and sisters in Christ. Then, and only then, will the "peace on earth" that the angels proclaimed become a reality.

(All participants — soloist, readers, and so forth — gather around and behind the manger. The pantomime characters remain in their places.)

Christmas Wishes
("Merry Christmas" is called out by all vocalists in their respective foreign languages, and then in English by all.)

Special Music And Hymn   "Silent Night"
(The first verse is sung by the children, then each vocalist sings a verse in his/her respective language. The last two verses are sung in English by the congregation. During the congregational singing, the children recess, preferably through a side exit.)

Sermon

Hymn   "It Came Upon A Midnight Clear"

Benediction
May the love of the Christ child fill your hearts and guide your actions. Go in his peace.

Benediction Response   "Let There Be Peace On Earth"

Postlude

4

What Is His Name?

A Children's Christmas Pageant
By Mary Lu Warstler

Notes

This Christmas program is written for children or for the total congregation's participation. In its flexibility any congregation, regardless of its size, can experience anew the telling of the story of the birth of Jesus, as well as relate the Christmas story to today's world.

Characters

The characters in this drama include many or few, depending on the size of your congregation.

The CHOIR can be any size or age, or a solo voice may be used. The song "What Is His Name?" is a simple melody which is sung in unison. The director may choose to have certain sections sing various verses or the entire choir may sing all of them.

The NARRATOR should be an adult, possibly the minister, who can speak clearly and with feeling. Mature teens can also do a good job. If you have a very large group with many persons who want speaking parts, the narrator's part can be divided among several people.

The INSTRUMENTAL SOLO can be any instrument which is available. However, a lower-pitched instrument such as an alto sax, trombone, or viola is preferable. If you have several possibilities, use a duet, trio, or other combination which give children a chance to share their talents.

The SLAVES, SHEPHERDS, POOR PEOPLE, KINGS, and SOLDIERS are all played by children in grades one through six. The props used by each can be made in Church School classes, beginning several weeks before time for the play to be presented. Or you could have a special costume-making party when all props would be made on the same day. If you have a very small church, one person in each category will work very well.

The ANGELS are traditionally the preschool and kindergarten children. They come in at the end of the program. They do not have to be on stage very long, since it is often very difficult for the little ones.

MARY and JOSEPH could be either adults or teens or older elementary children.

The BABY could be a life-sized doll wrapped in a blanket.

Costumes

The traditional look is in order. Mary, Joseph, shepherds, and kings may all wear robes with appropriate head dress. Poor people wear tattered, ragged modern-day clothes. Soldiers wear army-type uniforms of modern day or a combination of fighting clothes from several centuries if you have several persons in this category. The angels should have white robes, and wings (halos are optional but can be made from tree trimmings). The slaves may be dressed in modern clothes with chains of paper wrapped around them, especially draped over their arms.

At least one shepherd needs to have a toy lamb (or one made from cotton or pillow stuffing) to place before the manger. The kings will place their crowns and their gifts there. Poor persons will leave a tattered shawl. Soldiers will leave their weapons. Angels will leave stars which can be made of cardboard and aluminum foil. The slaves will leave their chains.

Setting And Scenery

The entire program takes place in the stable with Mary and Joseph and the baby Jesus. Each group is added to the stage until finally the angels complete the scene.

Mary should be seated on a small stool or chair in the center of the stage with Joseph standing beside her on her left. The manger with the baby should be directly in front of and between them. They both look at the manger during the program until the end when Mary picks up the baby and stands beside Joseph. Each group in turn approaches this scene while the choir sings the verse pertaining to them. They stop in front of the manger, facing it until the narrator finishes. Then they lay down their token and move behind Mary and Joseph until all are present. The angels are the last to enter. They stay in front of the manger, sitting on the floor so they do not hide the baby.

The choir can be at one side of the scene and the Narrator on the other.

Congregation Participation

Only one verse of most of the carols is used. (More can be used if you so desire. Most people know the words to the first verse, so you would not have to use books.) If you will not be using a bulletin, the responsive reading may be done by the Narrator and the Choir or by two other participants.

Order Of Service

Prelude

Words Of Welcome And Announcements

Opening Prayer   Narrator

Carol   "It Came Upon A Midnight Clear"

Offering

Carol   "Silent Night"
                                                       (two verses)
                        Mary and Joseph Enter

Narrator   Luke 2:1-7

Choir   "What Is His Name?"
                                                       (verse one)
                              Slaves Enter
Narrator

Carol   "While Shepherds Watched Their Flocks"
                                                        (one verse)

Narrator   Luke 2:15-16

Choir   "What Is His Name?"
                                                       (verse two)
                            Shepherds Enter

Narrator

Responsive Reading

    Leader: Blessed are the poor in spirit,

    People: For theirs is the kingdom of heaven.

    Leader: Blessed are those who hunger and thirst for righteousness,

    People: For they shall be satisfied.

Choir   "What Is His Name?"

                                                            (verse three)

Poor Persons Enter

Narrator

Instrumental Solo   "We Three Kings"

Narrator   Matthew 2:1-2

Poem   "Gifts For The King"

Choir   "What Is His Name?"

                                                           (verse four)

Kings Enter

Narrator

Carol   "Hark! The Herald Angels Sing"

                                                           (one verse)

Choir   "What Is His Name?"

                                                           (verse five)

Soldiers Enter

Narrator

Carol   "Angels We Have Heard On High"

                                                   (verses one and four)

Choir	"What Is His Name?"
	(verse six)

Angels Enter

Narrator

Children	"Away In A Manger"
Choir	"What Is His Name?"
	(verse seven)
Narrator	Luke 2:19
Carol	"Joy To The World"
	(all verses)

Benediction

Postlude

What Is His Name?

Characters
Mary
Joseph
A manger with a baby (doll) in it
Slaves with chains
Shepherds with sheep
Poor people with tattered, ragged clothes
Kings with crowns
Soldiers with weapons
Angels with stars
Choir*
Narrator*
Congregation*
Instrumental solo*

*Indicates speaking or musical parts. All others are nonspeaking.

Prelude (CHOIR *takes its place*)

Words Of Welcome And Announcements

Opening Prayer   Narrator
    As we gather this night to celebrate the birth of your Son, O
God, we ask that you will renew within each of us that spirit of
Christmas which the shepherds felt and that filled the angels with
song. May we name the Christ within our hearts this night. Amen.

Carol   "It Came Upon A Midnight Clear"

Offering (*Optional*)

Carol   "Silent Night"
(*Sing two verses while* MARY *and* JOSEPH *take their places.*)

Narrator

O listen this day to the story we tell,
A story so old, yet so new.
A baby was born in Bethlehem.
Words of the prophets come true.

(Read) Luke 2:1-7

Choir   "What Is His Name?"
                                             (verse one)

What is his name, this Babe in a manger?
What shall we call him? What is his name?

(SLAVES begin to move toward the manger holding their chains.)

We shall call him Lord,
Because we are slaves.
Oh . . . .
His name shall be Lord.

Narrator *(Optional: may be read by one of the slaves.)*
Slaves. We are slaves. We are in bondage to sin. We are in bondage to self — to bad habits. We are in prisons of our own making.
Let us all call him Lord, and loose our chains of bondage, freeing
ourselves to love. Lord, we give you our chains. Make us free.

*(SLAVES lay their chains down by the manger and move to the
background.)*

Carol   "While Shepherds Watched Their Flocks'
                                             (verse one)

Narrator   Luke 2:15-16

Choir   "What Is His Name?"
                                             (verse two)

What is his name, this Babe in a manger?
What shall we call him? What is his name?

(SHEPHERDS *come forward to the manger, at least one of them carrying a toy lamb.*)

We shall call him Shepherd.
Like sheep we all stray.
Oh . . . .
His name shall be Shepherd.

Narrator *(Optional: may be read by one of the shepherds.)*
We are shepherds, but so many times we act like sheep. We wander near and far. Like sheep, we are gentle and kind, but like sheep, we are prone to wandering. We aren't really bad most of the time, but we just nibble ourselves out of the pasture. When we are needed or when the flock is counted, we are not there. We wait for the shepherd to lead us back to where we really want to be. Let us call him Shepherd, and lay our lives at his feet, listening for his voice. Let us call him Shepherd.

(SHEPHERDS *lay their lamb by the manger and move to the background.*)

Responsive Reading *(Optional: Narrator and Choir may do this.)*
　　Leader: Blessed are the poor in spirit,
　　People: For theirs is the kingdom of heaven.
　　Leader: Blessed are those who hunger and thirst for righteousness,
　　People: For they shall be satisfied.

Choir　　　　　　　　　　　　　　　　"What Is His Name?"
　　　　　　　　　　　　　　　　　　　　　　(verse three)
What is his name, this Babe in a manger?
What shall we call him? What is his name?

(POOR PEOPLE *wearing ragged clothes with patched shawls or jackets enter and move toward the manger.*)

45

We shall call him Savior,
Because we are poor.
Oh . . . .
His name shall be Savior.

Narrator *(Optional: one of the poor folks may read.)*
We do not understand how so many of us poor exist in a world of
plenty. Jesus did not say that we have to be poor. He only stated a
fact, that there will always be poor folks. Sometimes through our
own foolishness or sin we bring poverty upon ourselves, but most
of us are victims of circumstances, environment, or birth. We just
happened to be born in the wrong place. Poverty will never change
without a Savior, so here is our gift. Let us all call him Savior.

*(POOR PERSON lays shawl by the manger and moves to the back-
ground.)*

Instrumental Solo   "We Three Kings"
                                                   (one or two verses)

Narrator   Matthew 2:1-2

Poem   "Gifts For The King"
The star pierced the darkness,
And shattered the night;
New hope dawned and sparkled,
As they followed its light.

Many miles they traveled
Over mountain and sea;
Bringing gifts for the King —
The King foretold to be.

Choir   "What Is His Name?"
                                                        (verse four)

What is his name, this Babe in a manger?
What shall we call him? What is his name?

(KINGS move toward the manger carrying their gifts.)

We shall call him King of kings,
We bring him our gifts.
Oh . . . .
His name shall be King of kings.

Narrator *(Optional: one of the kings may read.)*
We are kings. Kings of important countries. We have traveled very far to see a true King. We have brought him gifts of gold, frankincense, and myrrh, but we are really bringing him much more. No one can rule without good advice. No one can love well without loving and respecting someone higher. We love, honor, and respect the one who sent this child, therefore, we love, honor, and respect the One who is sent. We are only shadows. Here is a true King of all kings. Let us call him King of kings.

(KINGS place their gifts and crowns by the manger and move to the background.)

Carol   "Hark! The Herald Angels Sing"
                                                   (verse one)

Choir   "What Is His Name?"
                                                   (verse five)
What is his name, this Babe in a manger?
What shall we call him? What is his name?

(SOLDIERS move toward the manger bearing their weapons.)

We shall call him Prince of Peace,
Of war we are weary.
Oh . . . .
His name shall be Prince of Peace.

Narrator *(Optional: one of the soldiers may read.)*

There shall be wars and rumors of wars. We represent all the men and women who have died, and who will die in the ceaseless, endless, life-shattering wars and violence of this earth. Nations against nations, we slaughter thousands. Race against race, we hurt and divide. Family against family, brother against brother, sister against sister, parent against child. The list of wars that rage among us is endless. Not all wars are fought with guns or tanks or missiles. Most are fought with tongues and ignorance. Let us give him our weapons. Let us call him Prince of Peace and let the healing of war's hurts begin. Let us all call him Prince of Peace.

(SOLDIERS lay their weapons down by the manger and move to the background.)

Carol   "Angels We Have Heard On High"
                                              (verses one and four)

Choir   "What Is His Name?"
                                                          (verse six)

What is his name, this Babe in a manger?
What shall we call him? What is his name?

(ANGELS move toward the manger.)

We shall call him Son of God,
We see him in glory.
Oh . . . .
His name shall be Son of God.

Narrator

We worship him as Son of God. We watch with love and compassion as he takes the form of humankind. We wait, hovering close, ready for the command to pick him up if he falls, to feed him if he hungers, to minister to him in any way. We believe that this one who is chosen to be his Mother will love him. She will protect him as long as she can. We will always be ready to step in if necessary. He is our own King. Our own Son of God. We leave a symbol of our presence and call him Son of God.

48

(ANGELS lay their stars by the manger.)

Children   "Away In A Manger"

Choir   "What Is His Name?"
                                                        (verse seven)
What is his name, this Babe in a manger?
What shall we call him? What is his name?

(MARY picks up the baby and holds him close to her as she stands next to JOSEPH through the rest of the program.)

He shall be called Shepherd, Savior, King of kings,
Prince of Peace, Son of God. I shall call him Jesus.

Narrator   Luke 2:19

Carol   "Joy To The World"
                                                         (all verses)

(CHILDREN begin to exit on the second verse, followed by the CHOIR, followed by the NARRATOR, who gives the benediction from the back of the room. CHILDREN and CHOIR should stand quietly at the back until the benediction is given, then they can be first in line for cookies, if you care to serve refreshments.)

Benediction   Narrator
By whatever name you call this infant of Bethlehem, take him into your home, into your heart and soul. May he be yours. May you know the peace and joy of this Christmastime, because you indeed know the Christ of Christmas. Amen.

Postlude

WHAT IS HIS NAME?

Mary Lu Warstler

Adagio ♩ =72

(Chorus) What is his name?...... This Babe in a man - ger?
(verse 7) He shall be called Shep- herd, Sav - ior, King of kings

What shall we call him? What is his name?....
Prince of Peace, Son of God. I shall call him Je - sus.

1. We shall call him Lord, Be - cause we are slaves.
2. We shall call him Shep -herd, Like sheep we all stray,

Oh.............................. His name shall be Lord.....
Oh.............................. His name shall be Shep - herd.

Verses 3-6 of Song

3. We shall call him Savior,
   Because we are poor.
   Oh . . . .
   His name shall be Savior.

4. We shall call him King of kings,
   We bring him our gifts.
   Oh . . . .
   His name shall be King of kings.

5. We shall call him Prince of Peace,
   Of war we are weary.
   Oh . . . .
   His name shall be Prince of Peace.

6. We shall all him Son of God,
   We see him in glory.
   Oh . . . .
   His name shall be Son of God.

5

Come To The Manger

A Christmas Eve
Candlelight Communion Service

By Mary Lu Warstler

Christmas Eve Worship Service

Introit   Choir

Prelude   Organist
Let us quiet ourselves to hear God speak.

Service Of Acolytes

Call To Worship   Pastor and Liturgist

Prayer   In Unison
We come to the manger this night, O Lord, to behold the birth
once again. Let the wonder of that night so long ago fill us anew
with reverence and awe. Amen.

Hymn   "Angels We Have Heard On High"

Welcome And Greeting

Dialogue Of Angels   Pastor and Liturgist

Hymn	"O Little Town Of Bethlehem"
Dialogue Of Angels	Pastor and Liturgist
Anthem	Choir
Dialogue Of Angels	Pastor and Liturgist
Hymn	"What Child Is This?"
Dialogue Of Angels	Pastor and Liturgist

Service Of Holy Communion

Prayer Before Communion	Pastor
Distribution Of Elements	
Prayer After Communion	Liturgist
Call To Stewardship	Pastor
Offertory	
Giving Of Tithes And Offerings	
Choral Response	In Unison

(Chorus of "Angels We Have Heard On High")
Gloria in excelsis Deo,
Gloria in excelsis Deo.

Prayer Of Dedication	Liturgist
Dialogue Of Angels	Pastor and Liturgist
Hymn	"Silent Night"

Lighting Of Candles
*(Please dip the **unlit** candle toward the **lit** candle to avoid dripping hot wax. Please be very careful with small children.)*

Benediction   Pastor

Choir Response

Postlude   Organist

Come To The Manger

Introit Choir

Prelude Organist
Let us quiet ourselves to hear God speak.

Service Of Acolytes

Call To Worship Pastor and Liturgist
Pastor: Come to the manger, Shepherds, come.
Come and leave your sheep there.
Come to the manger, Shepherds, come.
Come see the babe asleep there.

Liturgist: Come to the manger, Angels, come.
Come sing your lullaby there,
Come to the manger, Angels, come,
Come, fill the starlit sky there.

Pastor: Come to the manger, People, come.
Come kneel before the King there.
Come to the manger, People, come.
Come lift your voice and sing there.

Prayer In Unison
We come to the manger this night, O Lord, to behold the birth once again. Let the wonder of that night so long ago fill us anew with reverence and awe. Amen.

Hymn "Angels We Have Heard On High"

Welcome And Greeting

Dialogue Of Angels Pastor and Liturgist
(Pastor is Angel 1 and Liturgist is Angel 2.)

Angel 1: Look! There are the shepherds on the hill watching their sheep. It is time. Let us go tell them the news.

Angel 2: But won't they be frightened?

Angel 1: We'll tell them not to be afraid.

Angel 2: Do you think they will hear us?

Angel 1: Of course they will hear us.

Angel 2: But what if they don't do as we tell them to do?

Angel 1: Don't worry. They will hear. They will follow our instructions.

Angel 2: But what if ...

Angel 1: Look! We don't worry about "what ifs." God said, "Go tell the shepherds." That is our mission. They must listen. Now, let's go. Oh, yoo-hoo! Shepherds!

Angel 2: See, I told you they would be afraid.

Angel 1: Don't be afraid, shepherds. We are here to bring you some good news.

Angel 2: Yes, God's Messiah is born in Bethlehem this very night.

Angel 1: In a stable behind the inn. Come, shepherds, to the manger and worship the Lord's Messiah.

Angel 2: Here come the host of angels to help us sing.

Hymn   "O Little Town Of Bethlehem"

Dialogue Of Angels   Pastor and Liturgist

Angel 1: Come now, shepherds. Come to Bethlehem. Come to the manger and see the child asleep there on that bed of hay.

Angel 2: Don't be afraid. God is with us. Emmanuel has come. Mary and Joseph have traveled far to reach Bethlehem.

Angel 1: Leave your sheep. They will be safe. Come, see the Holy Child. Be the first to worship at his manger bed.

Anthem   Choir

("Christmas Grace" or other suitable anthem)

Dialogue Of Angels   Pastor and Liturgist

Angel 2: Look! They are going to Bethlehem. They are not afraid anymore. How did you know they would go?

Angel 1: I just knew. Besides, God told me it was important. So I figured God knew how to get them there. He told me what to say.

Angel 2: But do we have to stay here and watch their sheep until they return?

Angel 1: We told them they would be safe, didn't we?

Angel 2: Yes, but this could get boring.

Angel 1: Not if you are doing your job. Grab that little one wandering away from the fold.

Angel 2: Ooops! I see what you mean. Guess I better keep my eyes open.

Angel 1: And ears. Listen! I hear a wolf creeping through the brush. I'll get him … There. No mutton chops for him tonight.

Angel 2: Shouldn't the shepherds be returning? Don't we have some other errands to do tonight?

Angel 1: Yes, I think I hear them returning now. They surely sound excited. They will tell stories all night. Come, let us go to the manger and see what is happening there.

Hymn   "What Child Is This?"

Dialogue Of Angels   Pastor and Liturgist

Angel 2: Isn't he a beautiful baby? And look how tenderly Mary wraps him in swaddling cloths.

Angel 1: I will never forget her expression when I told her she would bear God's Son.

Angel 2: What did she say?

Angel 1: At first she was much perplexed by my words.

Angel 2: What did you say to her?

Angel 1: I said, "Greetings, favored one! The Lord is with you."

Angel 2: And she was afraid of you, I bet — like the shepherds.

Angel 1: Yes, and I said, "Do not be afraid, Mary, for you have found favor with God." And then I told her she would bear God's Son and call him Jesus.

Angel 2: Did she question you?

Angel 1: Yes. She wondered how that could be since she was a virgin. But I told her the Holy Spirit would come upon her and the power of the Most High would overshadow her; therefore the child would be holy.

Angel 2: He is a beautiful baby. He will be great. He will be called the Son of the Most High and God will give him the throne of his ancestor David.

Angel 1: Yes, but there will be much sorrow before that happy day.

Angel 2: What do you mean?

Angel 1: Shhh! Listen. Someone is coming to the manger.

Angel 2: It is the people of the world.

Angel 1: Yes,
Come, people, come to the manger bed;
    See the Christ asleep there;
Come to his table to be fed,
    See the Christ alive there.

Remember how these words he spoke,
    The night he was betrayed:
"Eat this bread — my body broke,"
    Then in the tomb was laid.

"Remember, too, I'll be lifted up,
    And giving all for you;
So drink the contents of this cup,
    In remembrance that I love you."

From the time that tiny infant lay
    Upon his manger bed;
His life became a ransom pay,
    His blood for us was shed.

So come to the manger, People, come,
    Look beyond that day, there,
To the God who gave us his Son
    Life eternal with him to share.

Service Of Holy Communion

Prayer Before Communion   Pastor

Lord, God of all creation, you gave us Jesus, who was laid in a manger, crucified upon a cross, laid in a tomb, and raised from the dead — all that we may have life. And as though that were not enough, you gave us bread and wine that we might remember. May they be for us this night the body and blood of your Son, our Lord, as we remember anew. Amen.

Distribution Of Elements

Come feast at the Lord's Table in celebration of his birth, his death, his resurrection.

Prayer After Communion   Liturgist

Thank you for the feast given, for the remembrances of our hearts, for the forgiveness renewed, for the fellowship together around your table of love. Amen.

Call To Stewardship   Pastor

Come to the manger now, people of God. Bring your gifts to him with love and gratitude.

Offertory
Giving Of Tithes And Offerings

Choral Response   In Unison
(Chorus: "Angels We Have Heard On High")
    Gloria in excelsis Deo,
    Gloria in excelsis Deo.

Prayer Of Dedication   ·   Liturgist

O God, on this night when we celebrate the birth of your Son, Jesus, we bring you gifts of silver and paper, but beyond the gifts of money are the gifts of our hearts. Use all in telling your story to the world. Amen.

Dialogue Of Angels   Pastor and Liturgist
Angel 1: Look how the stars twinkle this night.

61

Angel 2: And especially the one bright star shining over the stable.

Angel 1: He will be the light of the world.

Angel 2: I wonder if the light will ever go out.

Angel 1: Not as long as people come to the manger and renew the spark of light in themselves.

Angel 2: Come to the manger, People, come,
   Never take your duty lightly
Come to the manger, People, come,
   Light your candles brightly.

Hymn "Silent Night"

Lighting Of Candles
*(Please dip the **unlit** candle toward the **lit** candle to avoid dripping hot wax. Please be very careful with small children.)*

Benediction Pastor
We have come to the manger this night, worshipped the child, fed at his table, taken his light. Let us now go into the world as the People of God, lighting the way in a world of darkness.

   Go in peace. May God go with us. Amen.

Choir Response

Postlude Organist

6

Mary: After The Angel

A Christmas Play
By Arlys M. Winkler

Notes

This play explores the thoughts and feelings of Mary, her peers, her parents, and Joseph as they learn that Mary is expecting a child. Each act takes place in someone's house, making the changing of props simple (for example: different tablecloths would signal a change of location). Programs could provide scene changes as well. Simple wooden tables and stools and costuming of the period are all that is needed. All scripture quotes are from the *New Revised Standard Version of the Bible*.

Characters

Mary	Anne
Joseph	Joachim
Deborah	Elizabeth
Judith	Narrator 1
Esther	Narrator 2

Special Instructions For Scene IV

The "moonlight" could be a spotlight or something as simple as a flashlight or candle.

Mary: After The Angel

NARRATOR 1: "In the sixth month, the angel Gabriel was sent by God to a town in Galilee called Nazareth, to a virgin engaged to a man whose name was Joseph, of the house of David. The virgin's name was Mary" (Luke 1:26-27).

NARRATOR 2: We join Mary now as she comes to the house of Deborah. Several days have passed since the angel's visit. Mary's friends, Deborah, Esther, and Judith, sit on stools, their heads together, whispering, as Mary enters.

Act I

(Curtain opens)

MARY: Shalom, my friends.

JUDITH: Shalom, Mary. Where have you been these last few days? We haven't seen you at the well or in the marketplace.

DEBORAH: *(Stands up and says sarcastically)* Yes, Mary, we were just talking about you. Where *have* you been?

MARY: *(Stammers)* I, I've been at home. I haven't been feeling well.

DEBORAH: *(Laughing)* What's the matter, Mary, have you been sick in the mornings?

ESTHER: *(Angrily)* Deborah, don't be so hateful. *(Stands, turns to* MARY *and puts her arm around her.)* What's wrong? Can we help?

MARY: *(Sits down)* Oh, Esther, you aren't going to believe this. I'm going to have a baby.

JUDITH: We heard.

MARY: *(Surprised)* You heard? Who told you?

DEBORAH: Veronica.

MARY: *(Disgusted)* Veronica? She promised me she wouldn't tell anyone.

JUDITH: Well, she sure told us.

ESTHER: Don't worry, Mary, I threatened her — she'll have to answer to me if she tells anyone else. I think she'll hold her tongue.

MARY: I hope so. I haven't told my parents yet ... or Joseph. I want to be the one to tell them. I don't want them to hear it from the gossips in our village.

DEBORAH: What are you waiting for? You won't be able to hide it forever.

ESTHER: Deborah, if you can't be nice, we're going to leave. Please, Mary needs us. Put yourself in her place. How would you feel?

JUDITH: I agree, Deborah; please don't be so nasty.

DEBORAH: *(Puts hands on hips)* Well, I'm just trying to be real-istic.

MARY: You're right. I'm going to tell them tonight. I haven't told them yet because I was trying to think of the best way. *(She shakes her head.)* But there just isn't a best way.

DEBORAH: Who's the father?

JUDITH and ESTHER: *(Together)* Deborah!

MARY: No, no, that's all right. It's an honest question. I'll give you an honest answer. *(She pauses and swallows, hard.)* The Holy Spirit. *(All three girls look incredulous.)*

DEBORAH: *(Laughs)* Mary, you're going to have to invent a better story than that. No one will believe you.

JUDITH: The Holy Spirit … Oh, sure. Right. *(Sarcastically)* Everyone will believe that.

ESTHER: Girls, girls, give her a chance to explain. *(They wait, expectantly.)*

MARY: It gets even more unbelievable.

ESTHER: What do you mean?

MARY: I was told this by — by an angel. (MARY *stands and all three girls sit down.)*

ESTHER: I think you'd better start at the beginning.

MARY: *(Pacing)* I was alone at prayers the other night and I, I heard a voice.

JUDITH: *(Deadpan)* Oh, sure … a voice.

MARY: I did. You have to believe me. You know what kind of a person I am. You know how very much I love God, how devoted I am to Him and His commandments. *(Pleading)* I'm not making this up. An angel came to me and told me I'm going to have a boy baby and Joseph and I are to name him Jesus and we are to raise him.

JUDITH: And Joseph is going to agree to this?

MARY: *(Quietly)* He loves me.

JUDITH: But does he love you enough to accept someone else's child? Will he believe you when you tell him what you've just told us?

DEBORAH: *(Sarcastically)* Why don't you just tell us who the father is, Mary? Tell us the truth.

MARY: *(Faces them squarely)* I have told you the truth. The angel told me not to be afraid, that the power of the Most High would overshadow me and I would conceive and bear a son, whom we are to call Jesus. I intend to do just as the angel said. Most of all, I'm going to try to not be afraid.

DEBORAH: What does overshadow mean?

MARY: *(Exasperated)* Deborah, I don't have any idea. There is so much I don't understand, but I'm sure eventually all will become clear. The angel told me that I had found favor with God. I have to believe that and trust that He will guide and protect me.

ESTHER: *(In awe)* Does God have special plans for this child you are going to have?

MARY: The angel said —

DEBORAH: *(Sarcastic again)* There's that old angel again.

JUDITH: Quit interrupting her.

MARY: The angel said that the child will be God's son. *(The three girls are stunned into a moment of silence.)*

ESTHER: *(Goes to MARY and takes her hands in hers)* Mary, are you sure you heard right?

MARY: *(Resolutely)* I am positive.

DEBORAH: Well, I don't believe anything you've told us. I think you're making it all up.

MARY: That's up to you, Deborah. I can't make you believe me.

ESTHER: I believe you, Mary. I really do.

MARY: What a relief. At least somebody does.

JUDITH: I want to believe you. Tell me again, what exactly did the voice say?

MARY: I'm going home to tell my parents. If you want to walk with me, you are welcome. I'll tell you more on the way. I need to remember everything. If I go over it and over it I'll be more calm when I tell them. *(ESTHER, JUDITH, and MARY start to leave.)*

MARY: *(Turns back)* Deborah, won't you come with us? *(DEBORAH turns away from them. MARY sadly shrugs, links her arms with ESTHER and JUDITH and they exit.)*

(Curtain closes)

Act II

Anne and Joachim's house

(Curtain opens. Mary's parents, ANNE and JOACHIM, sit at the table. ANNE is mending. JOACHIM is whittling as MARY enters.)

MARY: *(Clears her throat)* Mother. Father.

ANNE: Shalom, Mary dear. I was wondering where you were. It's almost time for our evening meal.

MARY: I was with Esther and Judith.

JOACHIM: Not Deborah? Isn't she always with you girls?

MARY: We had a disagreement.

ANNE: What about?

MARY: That's what I want to discuss with you.

JOACHIM: *(Puts down his knife and wood)* Sounds serious.

MARY: It is, Father. *(She begins pacing again.)* I don't know where to start.

ANNE: *(Gets up, goes to* MARY *and puts her hands on her shoulders)* The best place to start, dear, is at the beginning. *(She leads* MARY *back to a chair. They both sit down.)*

MARY: The other night I was praying. I, I was alone but, but, I heard a voice.

JOACHIM: You heard a voice?

MARY: Yes, Father. The voice told me he was an angel with a message from God. I was very frightened at first until the angel told me not to be afraid.

JOACHIM: What message did he bring, daughter?

MARY: *(Bows her head)* I'm going to have a baby.

JOACHIM: *(Jumps up and yells)* You're going to what?

MARY: Please, Father, don't yell. The angel told me the Holy Spirit would come upon me and I would have a son.

ANNE: *(Quietly)* Oh, Mary. *(Both* ANNE *and* JOACHIM *are momentarily stunned.)*

MARY: *(Goes to her knees in front of them, pleading)* Oh, Mother, Father, you know me. I keep God's laws, I wouldn't lie. As incredible as it sounds, I'm telling you the absolute truth.

JOACHIM: *(Says loudly)* I can't believe this.

ANNE: Joachim, please calm down. Hear Mary out. Let her finish.

MARY: Thank you, Mother. *(Begins again)* It's just as I said. The angel said his name was Gabriel. His first words were, "Rejoice, O highly favored daughter." He told me the Lord was with me and I would be blessed among women. I was so frightened, Father, I wanted to run away.

ANNE: But you didn't.

MARY: No, something kept me there and then I was filled with such a wonderful feeling of peace. I can't describe how good it felt. I — I didn't want to leave, I didn't want the angel to leave.

JOACHIM: *(Mellowing)* What else did — what'd you say his name was? Oh, yes, Gabriel. What else did Gabriel say?

MARY: Father, it was like a lovely dream. He said, "You will conceive and bear a son and you will name him Jesus. He will be great, and will be called the Son of the Most High."

ANNE: Mary, how can this be since you have not known a man?

MARY: Mother, that's exactly what I asked the angel.

JOACHIM: Well?

MARY: This is how he answered: "The Holy Spirit will come upon you, and the power of the Most High will overshadow you; therefore, the holy child to be born will be called Son of God."

ANNE: Oh, Mary.

JOACHIM: You are to become the mother of the Son of God? Impossible!

MARY: *(Humbly)* The angel said nothing is impossible with God. Father, you should know that. Look at Elizabeth and Zechariah. That's another thing the angel said. He reminded me about them, how they are going to have a child even though they are both so old.

ANNE: *(Excited now)* She's right, Joachim. Don't you remember? Zechariah has been mute ever since he had that vision. But, Elizabeth told us he'd made signs to her about that day and written on a writing tablet that an angel had visited him.

JOACHIM: Hmmm. And I seem to remember the angel's name was Gabriel.

MARY: *(Claps her hands in excitement)* Then you do believe me, Father?

JOACHIM: Mary, I don't know how we will be able to explain all this to our friends, but, yes, I believe you.

ANNE: And I, daughter. But, what about Joseph? Mary, you are betrothed to him. What will he say?

MARY: Mother, I don't know. I'm just going to have to trust God to help me. *(She laughs.)* Maybe God will send an angel to Joseph, too.

ANNE: When are you going to tell him?

MARY: I think I'll go see him after we eat.

JOACHIM: Do you want us to go with you?

MARY: *(Resolutely)* No, Father, this is something I have to do myself. *(They hug and begin to prepare the table for their evening meal.)*

(Curtain closes.)

Act III

Joseph's house

(Curtain opens. JOSEPH is sitting studying a scroll by candle-light as MARY enters.)

MARY: *(Softly)* Joseph.

JOSEPH: *(Looks up and comes to embrace her)* Mary, what a pleasant surprise. But, it's so late. Is something wrong? *(He pulls a stool near his and they sit holding hands.)*

MARY: Oh, Joseph, something has happened and I don't quite know how to tell you.

JOSEPH: Mary, we have been engaged for almost a year now. You know you can tell me anything. *(MARY hesitates. JOSEPH lifts her chin with his fingers and says gently)* Is it that bad, Mary?

MARY: *(Nods)* I'm going to have a baby.

JOSEPH: *(Stands up, stunned)* Mary, what are you saying?

MARY: Joseph, don't think the worst of me. Let me explain. An angel came to me and told me I am going to have a baby. I told the angel that couldn't possibly be. I've never been with a man. Joseph, you know that. As much as we love each other, we've never been together.

JOSEPH: Do you think me a fool, Mary? Everyone knows a woman has to know a man before she can be with child. *(Angrily)* Who have you been with?

MARY: Please, Joseph. You know me. I would never deceive you. I haven't been with anyone.

JOSEPH: Then how could you possibly be with child?

MARY: The angel said the Holy Spirit would come upon me.

JOSEPH: What does *that* mean? Mary, do you know how crazy that sounds? How can you expect me to believe that?

MARY: Joseph, you've studied the scrolls, you know the tremendous power of God. The angel told me the Most High would overshadow me and the holy offspring to be born will be called Son of God.

JOSEPH: *(Laughs)* You — you are going to conceive and bear the Son of God! You can sit there and tell me — me, Joseph, the man you are betrothed to, the man you are planning to receive as your husband — that you are going to have a child that isn't mine!

MARY: *(Gets up and goes to him)* Joseph, please, you must believe me.

JOSEPH: *(Slowly shakes his head)* No, Mary, I don't. *(He walks away from her.)* I think the best thing to do is to divorce you.

MARY: Divorce?

JOSEPH: Yes.

MARY: But, but what will everyone say?

JOSEPH: What will everyone say? What do you think everyone will say when they find out you are with child?

MARY: I don't care about anyone else. I only care about you, Joseph.

JOSEPH: What about your mother and father?

MARY: I've already told them and they believe me.

JOSEPH: Good. They can see you through this then. *(MARY starts to protest again. JOSEPH holds up his hands.)* It's settled. But, don't worry. I don't want to expose you to the law, so I will divorce you quietly. *(JOSEPH exits.)*

MARY: *(Calls after him)* Joseph, please, don't leave. *(She slumps down on a stool, sobbing.)*

(Curtain closes.)

Act IV

Anne and Joachim's house

(Curtain opens. MARY is sitting alone at her parents' table. JOSEPH enters.)

JOSEPH: Mary.

MARY: *(Looks up, startled)* Joseph?

JOSEPH: *(Goes to her and kneels in front of her)* Mary, can you ever forgive me?

MARY: *(Takes his head in her hands)* There's nothing to forgive. But what has happened to change your mind?

JOSEPH: I had a dream last night.

MARY: A dream?

JOSEPH: *(Nods)* At least I think it was a dream, but it was so real. An angel of the Lord appeared to me and told me I should not fear taking you as my wife, that it is by the Holy Spirit that you have conceived. The angel said you will have a son and I am to name him Jesus.

MARY: Oh, thank the Lord Most High. *(They embrace.)* I am so grateful that you finally believe me, Joseph.

JOSEPH: I am so sorry I doubted you.

MARY: *(Laughs)* Well, I have to admit, I really can't fault you for not believing me. The important thing is, you do believe me now. *(Pauses)* What else did your angel tell you?

JOSEPH: That all this would happen to fulfill what the Lord had said through the prophet: "The virgin shall conceive and bear a son, and they shall name him Emmanuel" (Matthew 1:23).

MARY: *(Softly)* And that convinced you?

JOSEPH: Yes.

MARY: Then you still want me as your wife?

JOSEPH: Yes.

MARY: You're not afraid of what lies ahead for us?

JOSEPH: *(Shakes his head)* No, are you?

MARY: Not if I have you by my side.

JOSEPH: *(Embraces her)* Every step of the way.

(Curtain closes.)

Act V

Zechariah's house

(Curtain opens. ELIZABETH is kneading bread on a table as MARY enters.)

MARY: Shalom, Elizabeth.

ELIZABETH: *(Places her hands on her stomach)* "Mary, blessed are you among women, and blessed is the fruit of your womb" (Luke 1:42).

MARY: *(Embraces her)* How did you know I'm with child?

ELIZABETH: *(Holds her at arms length, smiling)* "And why has this happened to me, that the mother of my Lord comes to me?" (Luke 1:43).

MARY: *(More urgently)* Elizabeth, tell me how you know!

ELIZABETH: "For as soon as I heard the sound of your greeting, the child in my womb leaped for joy" (Luke 1:44).

MARY: "The Lord has looked with favor on the lowliness of his servant. From now on all generations will call me blessed" (Luke 1:48).

ELIZABETH: "Blessed is she who believed that there would be a fulfillment of what was spoken to her by the Lord" (Luke 1:45).

MARY: But I am so afraid. The angel told me not to be, but I can't help it.

ELIZABETH: I'm a little frightened, too, Mary. To have a child at my age won't be easy.

MARY: I hope you don't mind my coming for a visit. You have always been so understanding and I really need someone to talk to now.

ELIZABETH: How is everyone taking the news?

MARY: Mother and Father were quite upset at first.

ELIZABETH: *(Nods)* Can you blame them? And Joseph?

MARY: He was going to divorce me quietly, but then an angel visited him, too. Now he is looking forward to our marriage once more.

ELIZABETH: Thank the Lord for sending His angel messengers!

MARY: I wish He'd send some to my friends.

ELIZABETH: Are they making it difficult for you?

MARY: *(Nods)* Very.

ELIZABETH: All of them?

MARY: No, not all. And I'm grateful for the friends who aren't condemning me. But, still the others point and whisper when I walk by … and that hurts.

ELIZABETH: *(Gathers MARY in her arms)* My sweet child, just ignore them. You have a loving family and your wonderful

Joseph to see you through this. *(Pauses)* And most of all you have the assurance of our loving Lord. You are doing exactly what the angel asked of you.

MARY: Well, at least I'm going to try.

ELIZABETH: Good. Now how long do you want to stay with us?

MARY: I'm not sure. I think I'll know when I'm ready to return home.

ELIZABETH: I think you're right. God is guiding you and will help you realize when that time comes.

MARY: In the meantime I hope I can be of some help to you.

ELIZABETH: *(Firmly)* You can. In fact, you can start right now by finishing kneading this bread for me. *(MARY washes her hands and starts kneading. ELIZABETH sits down, fanning herself with her apron.)*

ELIZABETH: Now, tell me everything, child, right from the beginning. What did the angel look like?

(Curtain closes as they visit.)

Act VI

Anne and Joachim's house

(Curtain opens. MARY is seated by a window, looking up and out. The room is in total darkness. A soft "moonlight" illuminates MARY as she prays.)

(Luke 1:49-55)

"The Mighty One has done great things for me, and holy is his name. His mercy is for those who fear him from generation to generation. He has shown strength with his arm; he has scattered the proud in the thoughts of their hearts. He has brought down the powerful from their thrones, and lifted up the lowly; he has filled the hungry with good things, and sent the rich away empty. He has helped his servant Israel, in remembrance of his mercy, according to the promise he made to our ancestors, to Abraham and to his descendants forever."

(Curtain closes.)

7

Christmas At Bethlehem And Beyond

A Worship Service And Choral Reading
By Lynda Pujadó

Call To Worship

L: Heavenly Father, by sending us your tiny son to be born in a Bethlehem countryside, you love us with an extreme, powerful humility and simplicity.

P: At this Christmas season which is often a time of rushing and pressure, help us to uncomplicate our lives, and to be gentle with ourselves and remember your Christmas example of our divine Savior in the most humble of surroundings.

L: With the birth of your son, angels appeared praising your name in glorious heavenly voices to the shepherds.

P: We belong to heaven's divine eternity, where Christ and the angels came from, although we live today in earth's reality, with man's problems and confusion. We know there is another realm, another dimension waiting for us where God lives, and where angels sing praises constantly, and where there is peace.

L: Oh God, your timing in the universe is always perfect. You control the universe. You controlled the star for the Wise Men. You control angels to do your will. They came to Mary, Joseph, the shepherds, and the Wise Men. You control all realms of existence.

P: Forgive our human doubts and fears about our lives. You are to be trusted and praised always. We are so small, but we are under your constant, caring, divine sovereignty.

L: You are a God who is a great giver of gifts.

P: During this Christmas, we ask to receive Christmas gifts you would have us receive: gifts of wisdom, strong integrity in our lifestyle, and renewed courageous faith in you, our Heavenly Father, Redeemer, and Protector, so that we may live our lives close to Bethlehem's manger and our Savior.

Psalm 148:1-5 *(Read responsively)*

New Testament Reading   1 Corinthians 13:1-13

Prayer Of The Church

Dear Heavenly Father,

As eternal Lord of the universe, you come to us in many ways in gentle kindness. You sent angels and revealed heaven's glory to the remote shepherds. You sent your messenger to Mary, an obscure young girl in a village. You spoke to Joseph and the Wise Men in dreams, proving you know the very thoughts in our minds and can interrupt them.

You sent the Wise Men a compelling, brilliantly lit, traveling star that outshone everything in the universe, and that went ahead of them, demanding a journey by faith into the unknown to find their Savior.

You gave us the best gift you could, your son, and yet placed him in the Bethlehem countryside, poor and in humble circumstances, devoid of any human standards of importance, proving that you are a God who desires sincere faith from us and not a God interested in worldly values of prestige and influences. Open our minds to the fact of your overwhelming Christmas love for us.

Like the star for the Wise Men, your son Jesus is our eternal star shining for us, always waiting for us and beckoning us to himself and eternal life. Let us take hold of Christ's example of simplicity and self-denial and reflect the glow of eternity with our own lights of faith, and servanthood in a world that is so needful of a Savior's love and salvation.

Help us to meet your son, the Prince of Peace, at the manger this Christmas.

In Jesus' name. Amen.

Christmas At Bethlehem And Beyond
(A five-part choral reading for Christmas)

Voice

1   She was a young girl.

2,3   Unimpressive.

3,4,5   Common, actually.

1,5   And, so was Nazareth.

2,3,4   Nothing important would come from that village!

5   Mary was Jewish, and like most young Jewish girls, knew about the coming of the Messiah.

4,5   It was a reality in their minds.

1,2,3   Their Messiah was coming!

4   Mary had been raised in a good home and had listened to sacred Scriptures while growing up.

1,3   As was the custom, Mary was betrothed.

2,4,5   Her parents had arranged it, and she would make a fine wife and mother.

3   She knew what was expected of her.

2,4   The engagement was binding, and serious according to Jewish law.

1,5   Joseph was a righteous man.

5   His ancestral lineage could be traced to King David of Jerusalem.

ALL   He was only a carpenter.

1,3,5   He lived his life honestly and according to strict Jewish customs.

1,4   He was getting married soon, and it would be a wedding in Nazareth, where they would live close to their families.

3,4,5   They had always lived in Nazareth.

4   Our holy God communicates with his people in many ways.

2,5   Sometimes, he speaks to them.

1,2,5   Sometimes, he communicates messages they need to know by way of dreams.

3   With Mary, God sent an angel named Gabriel to visit her.

4,5   The angel came to Nazareth.

1,3   He did not visit anyone else there.

84

2,3,4	He came to Mary directly.
1	They were alone when he spoke to her.
3,4	She heard her name spoken by Gabriel.
1,2,5	He had important things to tell her from God.
5	The angel was God's messenger.
2,3	The young girl was extremely concerned when he talked to her.
1,4	She didn't understand, at first, and it was hard to adjust to the situation.
2,3,5	The angel was a spiritual being and was surrounded in a supernatural, spiritual existence.
4	The angel told Mary she had been chosen by God for a purpose.
1,5	She could barely stand in the angel's presence. She was very afraid.
2,3,4	But she knew what he was saying. She understood him.
3	He continued to tell her about her future.
2,5	God had chosen her to bear the coming Messiah, the son of God, whose kingdom would have no end.
ALL	The child would be called Jesus.
2	It was the name God chose for his son.
2,4	Mary was not married and she wondered how this would be done.
1,3,5	The angel told her the divine power of the Holy Spirit would come upon her and she would conceive.

Suggested Musical Interlude   "Lo, How A Rose Is Growing"
verses 1 and 2

1	With the angel's commanding presence, Mary was immersed in holiness.
3,4	She wanted to be a woman approved of by God, and she wanted to do the will of God and said so.
2,3,5	But, she did not comprehend how it would be done.
1,4	The angel knew her thoughts and gave her a verse from God.

85

2	*"Nothing will be impossible with God"* (Luke 1:37, NRSV).
3,4	Before the angel left her, he told her about Elizabeth, her elderly cousin.
1,2,4	She was far too old to have a child and had always been barren.
ALL	God works miracles.
3	He knew the heart of Elizabeth, who had tried to be a righteous woman of God her entire life.
1,5	Now, Elizabeth was going to have a son.
2,3	He would be the forerunner of Christ.
1,4,5	God knew that it was important for Mary to know someone that could relate to divine, angelic intervention.
4	Elizabeth knew about it and Mary loved her cousin.
2,5	The angel swiftly left Mary.
2,4	He slipped back to an invisible and spiritual realm of existence.
5	His assignment with her was finished, and he left her alone with her thoughts.
1,3	There were many things that were hard to understand.
2,5	Life for her had changed drastically, and so suddenly.
1	It was difficult to comprehend the divine power of the Messiah she was to bear.
1,3,5	He was coming and she was not married.
2,4	It was a dangerous crime not to be married and to be expecting a baby.
1,5	She came from a good home and there would be a scandal.
2,3,4	Joseph would be deeply hurt. She could not explain this to Joseph!
3,4	Her parents would be saddened, and the parents of Joseph would be shocked at the girl who had been chosen for their son.
2	Mary of Nazareth, the young girl who was chosen by God, had a test of faith ahead of her.
3,5	The angel Gabriel did not tell her what she should do.
ALL	The angel Gabriel was gone now.

2,4,5	There was only silence where he had been.
2,3	He had come so fast!
1,5	All this came so unexpectedly.
2,4	There had been no warning.
1,4	There had been no indication that this would happen to her.
3,4,5	No one knew about this, except God.

Suggested Musical Interlude   "What Child Is This?"

verses 1 and 2

3	Mary kept everything the angel told her locked quietly inside her, and —
1,3	Immediately, she went to visit Elizabeth, who was expecting the baby promised to her by God.
5	Elizabeth was filled with the Holy Spirit when she met Mary.
4,5	It was a spiritual luxury that God bestowed on Elizabeth.
3,4	She was filled with the reality of God's presence when she was confronted with the person of Mary.
1,2,3	She knew Mary would be the mother of the Messiah.
2	She knew it inside herself, and —
3,4,5	She knew it because of God's spiritual witnessing to her.
4	In the home of Elizabeth, sacred, treasured Scripture verses flowed out of Mary, the way a lovely, hidden river suddenly is noticed flowing out of the earth.
1	And, to Elizabeth, the young Jewish woman from the small, insignificant village in Galilee described her deeply profound knowledge of God's character, her close relationship to him, and his personal concern for her.
3,5	It was a wellspring of fluent, eloquently spoken praises from Mary, who had been raised in a home where Jehovah God, Scripture, and religion were respected, and assumed to be an integrated part of everyday life.
2,3,4	Mary said God's name was holy, meaning that his name was also all-powerful.

1,2	Mary said that God's opinion of people is different from that of the world's.
1,3,5	God loves humility and disdains those who are proud because they disrupt the quality of a person's character.
2,4	She talked about Abraham, the ancient man of faith, as if she had known him.
3,4	But, there were 42 generations between Mary of Nazareth and Abraham.
4	Nevertheless, it was the same God who communicated to both of them, and the same God who demanded from them a seemingly impossible death-defying faith.
ALL	It is the same God who communicates to his faithful today.
2	And, it is the same God who requires the seemingly impossible faith from those who love him.
2,3,5	Mary stayed in the home of her beloved cousin about three months.
1,5	When she left and went home to Nazareth, it was obvious that she was expecting a child.
2,4	In Nazareth, there was no one she could confide in about God's child, about the angel's visit to her, and divine intervention in her life.
1,3	Mary shared secrets with God, but she was in danger.
2,4,5	She did not know what to do, and she wondered silently about God's concern for her and the baby.
1,4	Had God forgotten her?

Suggested Musical Interlude   "Infant Holy, Infant Lowly"
                                                                verses 1 and 2

2,5	There was nothing she could do and her future husband was extremely upset.
3,4	Joseph decided to quietly divorce her.
1,2,5	He felt he had been so badly hurt that he had no other choice but to do that, although it was disturbing to him.
2,3	Divorce to him was not something that he had ever considered probable.

1,4,5	An important element of severe trust had been broken.
2,5	To him, their lives, and the lives of their families, had become shattered and broken like a fragile vase that falls and breaks into irreparable, innumerable pieces.
3,4	Mary had done it!
1,5	It was her fault!
4,5	It was impossible that this had happened, but it had.
3	While an angel of the Lord had appeared directly to Mary in person, he came to Joseph in a dream while he was asleep.
1,4	The angel from God talked to Joseph's mind and interrupted his thought patterns.
2,3	The angel explained about Mary being the mother of the Messiah.
4,5	The long awaited Old Testament prophecy was being fulfilled now:

"The virgin will be with child and will give birth to a son, and they will call him Immanuel," which means, "God with us" (Matthew 1:23, NIV).

2,3,5	The angel further explained to Joseph that he should not divorce Mary.
4	It was the same as if a special, personal friend had sat down and talked with him and opened his mind.
1,3	The carpenter was determined to protect Mary and allow no harm to come to her.
2,3,4	And Mary's life and the baby's were safe for the time being.
3	The Roman Caesar at that time was Caesar Augustus.
1,5	He decided to count the earth's population, and ordered a census.
2	After all, from his point of view, the population belonged to him.
1,2	Joseph was descended from King David who was from Bethlehem, so he had to go there with Mary and register.
3,4	There were 27 generations between King David and Joseph of Nazareth.
5	King David had loved his Lord, and he proved it.

1,2,4 Once, he proved it when he was only a shepherd.

1,3,5 Joseph had not needed to be concerned about God's honor, before this.

2,5 Like David, his ancestor, Joseph came from humble beginnings.

3,4 He was only a carpenter, and Nazareth was nothing anyone would think about.

4 Now, God had visited him so he would understand he was responsible for the safekeeping of Mary and her baby.

2,4,5 It was not his child.

Suggested Musical Interlude   "It Came Upon A Midnight Clear"
verses 1 and 2

4,5 No one knew the tremendous responsibility Joseph had.

1,3 He was more alone now than he had ever been before.

1,4 He could discuss this situation with no one.

2,5 He was not a wealthy man, nor did he have special provisions set aside for taking care of a sudden baby, the son of God.

3,4 He lived by the work of his hands.

1,2,3 He had always done this.

5 He was honest and reputable.

2,4 From Nazareth in Galilee to Bethlehem in Judea, it was about 60 miles, or about a three-day trip.

1,3 When they arrived, Bethlehem was busy.

3,5 It was very noisy.

2,4,5 There were many people there for the census and the local dwelling place was filled.

1,2,3 There were strangers crowding all over Bethlehem.

3,4 Joseph took Mary and went out to the countryside where it was peaceful.

5 It was quiet there, very still and beautiful.

ALL No one knew they were there.

1,5 They were so unimportant.

2,3 Mary was going to have her baby and there was no one to help her.

4	She did not have any family or friends near her.
1,2,4	She was so young.
3,5	Nearby, local shepherds stayed with their animals.
2,3,5	They did it everyday.
1,2,4	They often stayed awake at night if the animals were playing in the moonlight and wouldn't settle down and sleep.
1,4,5	They talked among themselves.
2,3	They had known each other for years and they were common, everyday people.
1,3	They were not important people, though.
2,4	They did not have high prestige in society.
5	They did not have political power, nor did they have money or any form of material prosperity.
1,2	They lived their lives day after day, doing just about the same things.

Suggested Musical Interlude "Angels From The Realms Of Glory"
verses 1 and 2

3,5	But, suddenly, as they were together, an immense aura of heaven's glory,
ALL	Bright, celestial light,
3,4	Beauty and tremendous goodness encompassed the men.
1,5	It was a powerful, overwhelming realm of existence from God.
2,3	They were not on earth, in the Bethlehem countryside, as much as they had been before.
4	They were in a spiritual realm with heavy, golden, flowing streams of light in the sparkling night's blackness.
ALL	It was coming down upon them.
2,5	Coming just for them, and for a while, heaven was with them.
3,4,5	And an angel was in front of the men.
1,3,4	They were frightened and wanted to hide because of the real power of the angel, and,
1,2	Because the shocking, searching light terrified them.
ALL	It seemed to know them too well!

3,4 It was a fear they had not known before.

1,5 Mary of Nazareth had been afraid when the angel Gabriel visited her, also.

1,2,3 They did not know what to do.

2,4 There was no place to escape this overwhelming love from God coming to them.

1,5 The angel said not to be afraid!

2,5 The angel spoke and gave the men an explicit message about the new baby.

4 The angel gave them information about their Messiah, Jesus, and where to find him:

1 *"Do not be afraid. I bring you good news of great joy that will be for all the people. Today in the town of David a Savior has been born to you; he is Christ the Lord. This will be a sign to you: You will find a baby wrapped in cloths and lying in a manger"* (Luke 2:10-12, NIV).

3,4 All the men listened to the angel and understood what was being said to them.

2,5 It was very hard to comprehend the angelic, supernatural intervention that was happening.

1,2,3 It was hard to adjust to this celestial sphere of experience.

2,4,5 Then, when the angel had finished speaking,

ALL Many angels appeared.

1,3,5 The sky exploded with them.

3 Massive amounts of glorious spiritual beings flooded the blackened night, and outshone the splendor of the stars in the universe which often bore down on Bethlehem like heavily weighted translucent, jeweled magnets.

4,5 All the shepherds saw the angels.

3,4 Heavenly angels, beings sent from God —

1,2,3 From God's home to these men who had never been special at any time —

3,5 Who had never known anything other than mere daily existence and,

1,2,4 Now they knew about an experience that transcended the physical boundaries of human consciousness.

1	In the midst of the shepherds, the crowding scene of angels praised God in delicately flowing, lilting, cascading, soothing, and melodious voices.
ALL	A myriad of voices.
2	Voices!
2,3,4	A cacophony of audible, luxurious voices!
ALL	Voices!
4	There were voices everywhere praising God ... but they were not of human origin.

Suggested Musical Interlude   "Hark! The Herald Angels Sing"
verses 1 and 2

4,5	The angels had been personally sent by God to the shepherds!
2,3	They said,
	"Glory to God in the highest, and on earth peace among men with whom He is pleased!" (Luke 2:14, RSV).
3,5	With supernatural peace, quietness, and deliberately profound silence, they immersed themselves back into the invisible heavenly place they came from,
2,4	And the shepherds were together again on the physical hillside with their animals.
1,5	They looked around.
2,3,5	The angels were not there.
1,4,5	They were not coming back.
2,5	And the shepherds were overcome with the ecstasy and glory of what had happened to them.
1,2	They decided to find the baby and also —
3,4	Tell the world about him!
3,4,5	They now knew that God knew them individually,
1	And cared about them to such an extent that they would always remember this attention and deep personal respect.
ALL	They were just shepherds!
1,3	After Mary had her tiny baby, she laid him down in the manger.
2,4	It was safe there, and Mary could rest.

2	She was very poor and had little for the new baby and there was no attention or special kindness given to her at all.
2,3	And she had the son of God, our eternal king, to take care of.

Suggested Musical Interlude　　　　　　　"Silent Night, Holy Night"
verses 1 and 2

1,2,3	The shepherds went searching.
4,5	They knew the countryside well.
2,4,5	They had traveled it continually, since it was part of their lives.
2,5	And they knew every manger and every farm nearby.
1,3	They found Mary and Joseph and told them about the angels.
2,3,4	In their excitement and great enthusiasm, they mirrored heaven's eternal glory.
2,5	They said what had been told to them about the child.
5	They saw the child and they marveled at him and could not stop their tumultuous, contagious joy at seeing the tiny baby.
3,4	Mary felt better when she saw and felt the shepherds' great awe and happiness at seeing Jesus.
1,2,4	Joseph felt less alone when the men came and extended to him their hearty greetings, and their knowledge of God's personal concern about them.
ALL	Mary would always remember this night,
2,4,5	She would remember the shepherds' visit and how kind they had been.
1,3	There was no one else to see the new baby.
3,5	Mary had a lot of private thoughts and she treasured them.
1,2	The shepherds returned to their jobs but exclaimed to anyone who entered their life about God's angels, about God's care, about Mary and Joseph, and the truth about the baby Jesus.
2,4	Their living, personal testimony inspired many people to think about and consider Jesus as their coming Messiah.

Suggested Musical Interlude   "Go Tell It On The Mountain"
                                       verses 1 and 2

1,5   After the child had been born in Bethlehem,
ALL   A star arose in the east.
2,4,5 It was not a normal star.
1,3   Its luminosity was intense.
2,5   It was larger than normal, and —
ALL   It traveled.
4,5   It seemed to have a definite journey that it was on sched-
          ule to take.
1,2   The star had a compelling aspect about it that no other star
          or star cluster had.
1,2,3 It could have been a comet, really.
2,4,5 The astronomers did not know what it actually was.
1,3   But they assumed that it represented the birth of a new
          king.
2,5   Nothing had ever demanded their attention like this be-
          fore!
1,4,5 Some astronomers felt they needed to follow it,
3   But this represented a tremendous journey into the un-
          known.
2,4   They didn't know where the star was going.
1,5   They didn't know how long it would take to follow it.
2,3   Besides, there were tremendous dangers on any long dis-
          tance journey.
3,5   There were difficult risks to take,
ALL   And maybe for nothing at all.
2,4,5 They would have to say good-bye to their families.
1,4   There was social criticism about their decision to follow
          something in the universe that no one else saw,
3,5   Or cared about.
2,3,5 A brightly moving object in the night sky was not a highly
          important item for anyone to consider.
2,4   But they did.
1   And they left their jobs, their homes, and their families to
          follow a star that demanded attention but did not wait for
          them.

2,3	Because they felt the new celestial object was meant to be the birth of a new king,
1,2	They took with them appropriate gifts to present to a king.
2,3,5	In the east, the growth, manufacture and international trade of frankincense was flourishing.
2,5	Tons of frankincense were exported from the east by way of camel caravans and shipping at sea.
3,4	It was a heavy, deeply intoxicating, luxurious perfume meant for the rich who could afford it.
2,4	The astronomers took frankincense with them for the new king they sought.
1,5	They took gold. There was gold in their country.
2,3	Gold was meant for kings.
1,4,5	And they took rough, expensive, perfumed balls of myrrh from their myrrh trees.
2,3,5	When they started to follow the star,
1,4	They soon faced loneliness.
2,3,4	They often faced disaster, but they kept going.
1,4	The star always went on ahead of them.
4,5	At night, away from their homes, they patiently studied and charted the star.
1,3	It was their companion.
ALL	It commanded them.
1,4	It demanded their faithfulness.
3	If they did not follow the star, it would be as though they had not been faithful to the calling of their heart —
1,2	Or faithful to the calling of something they could not deny, but did not understand.
3,5	They had not known a king to call them to himself like this before.
4,5	Not with a spectacular, supernaturally powered star, or whatever it was.
1,2,3	It was as though its course was predetermined by something they did not understand.

Suggested Musical Interlude   "The Hills Are Bare At Bethlehem"
verses 1 and 3

2,4,5	And after following the star for a long time, they came to the country of Judea.
2,3	It was a foreign country, with different customs and a different language.
5	They didn't know how they would be treated.
1,3,5	The star was abruptly stopped over the palace of King Herod in Jerusalem.
2,3	The astronomers were honored to visit the king and tell him of their plans.
ALL	They knew he would help them.
4	He was the king, and besides, he said he wanted to worship the king they sought, also.
3,4	It was strange that he didn't know any more about this king than they did.
1,2	He was not impressed with the star they had so diligently followed.
3,5	He did not even want to see it.
1,5	With enthusiasm, they explained to him that it was directly above his palace.
ALL	He did not move from his throne.
2,3,4	King Herod was Jewish, and considered the study of stars close to astrology, which was abhorrent to his Jewish religion.
4	When he needed an explanation for any type of phenomenon in the universe, he consulted the Pharisees,
4,5	And they consulted the sacred Scriptures.
1,3	The Pharisees found an ancient Scripture which they related to the king about a new king being born:
2,4	*"But you, Bethlehem Ephrathah, though you are small among the clans of Judah, out of you will come for me one who will be ruler over Israel, whose origins are from of old, from ancient times"* (Micah 5:2, NIV).
3,5	Because of the prophecy, the king sent the Wise Men on to the small town of Bethlehem.
1,5	It was only about five miles from Jerusalem.
1,2	They gladly promised to tell Herod when they found the new king.

3,4 After all, he was the king, and he had been so gracious to them —

1,5 So keenly interested in their mission.

2,4 He was to be respected, and

ALL They gave him their word.

Suggested Musical Interlude "Let All Together Praise Our God" verses 1 and 2

3,5 Herod knew he could easily keep track of the foreign men.

1,3,5 It would be hard for them to escape his soldiers.

1,4 King Herod had it made, politically speaking, with the men from the East.

3,4 He would easily get rid of them, soon, and whoever it was they were seeking as well.

2,5 Herod didn't need any opposition to his throne, and murder was a convenient political gesture for him.

1,2,3 Although he considered observing the patterns of the universe to be against his religion, murder was not.

1,3 To the Wise Men, Bethlehem didn't seem quite like the place for a king to be born.

2 They wondered if the star was wrong, again, as it had been over King Herod's palace in Jerusalem.

3,4,5 They had come so far, and had been alone for so long.

2,5 The star had always gone on ahead of them.

3 They had always followed it as though there were a tremendous need to do it.

3,4 There had been so much dedicated, blind trust on their part.

1,5 And now they were in Bethlehem, which was only a small, insignificant place.

ALL It was nothing, really.

2,4,5 Everything seemed a terrible mistake.

1,4,5 It seemed as though they had given up everything for nothing!

2,3,5 The star seemed to be directly above a small home in the village.

98

1,4	The people were exceptionally normal, and common.
2,3	Joseph was only a carpenter and Mary, his wife, was very young.
1	They explained that their child was the Messiah, the eternal king of kings.
2,5	Hundreds of years earlier, the prophet Isaiah had foretold the birth of Jesus and he said:
1	*"For to us a child is born, to us a son is given; and the government will be upon his shoulder, and his name will be called 'Wonderful Counselor, Mighty God, Everlasting Father, Prince of Peace' "* (Isaiah 9:6, RSV).
1,5	The astronomers had been led by the star to a child.
4	They were led to the son of God and to a man of eternity.
3,5	The astronomers from the east had met their Savior and they immediately worshipped him.
1,4	They gave him their gifts and were filled with peace, joy, and adoration.
2,4,5	They had found what they had been seeking.
1,4	They found eternal peace and their personal Savior.
2,3	Now they could return to King Herod and tell him the good news of Jesus Christ, son of God and Messiah.
1,5	But, like Joseph who didn't know any better when he planned to divorce Mary,
2,3,4	God warned the Wise Men about Herod's evil intentions toward them.
1,3	They would have to avoid him and quickly return to their country by a different route.
ALL	God did it in a dream,
2,4	And he did it immediately.
1,4	He came into their minds and affected their thoughts.
1,2	He showed extreme care to the astronomers, who didn't know he was watching them follow the star he directed.
ALL	All alone he was watching them.

Suggested Musical Interlude   "Angels We Have Heard On High"

verses 1 and 3

4	God's eyes followed them from their home, along the dangerous path of the star, into the palace in Jerusalem, and then to Bethlehem.
2,3,5	God watched them worship his son.
1,2,3	King Herod was coming to Bethlehem.
ALL	He was coming soon!
1,4	He was coming with his soldiers to kill the child, the parents, and the wise astronomers.
2,5	In the night, God also strongly and emphatically intervened in the mind of Joseph, as he had done before.
2,3	He told him to leave Bethlehem and go to Egypt.
1,4	They had to leave immediately.
3,5	There was no time to say good-bye or to gather extra provisions.
1,2,5	There was no time for personal feelings or sentiments.
3,4,5	They only had time for the present, for the extreme moment.
ALL	They had to leave at once.
1,3,4	God said so!
2,4	Herod was coming with his army ready to kill them all.
2,5	He gave orders to kill the Jewish infants two years old or younger.
3	Now Mary of Nazareth and her husband, a carpenter from an obscure village, were wanted by King Herod as enemies of the state.
1,4	In Egypt, they would be safe.
2,3,4	Herod's jurisdiction did not go into Egypt.
ALL	God had known that.
1,2,4	Egypt was so far away.
4	Mary wondered where they would end up, and if she would ever see her home in Nazareth again.
4,5	Mary and Joseph did not know how they would be treated there.
1,4	They had to trust God for their lives, and for everything.
2,3	Mary held the baby tightly.
4,5	Quickly, they fled into the safety of the night's darkness.
3,4	It surrounded them, protected them, and accepted them.

2,5   They were so poor! They had so little!

1,5   And they walked side by side with extreme danger.

2,3,5   They walked side by side, holding onto God's extended hand of kindness.

4   But shattering, earsplitting screams were heard all over Bethlehem.

1,3   Mothers ran, frantically trying to avoid Herod's soldiers.

2   They were killing the Jewish baby boys so the new king would be eliminated.

2,3   The soldiers, heavy men with swords and sharp spears who knew treacherous combat as their profession, were paid to kill innocent, sleeping infants.

ALL   It was just their job.

4,5   They were paid to hunt a tiny child named Jesus and his parents.

2,3,4   But they could not find them.

3   Mary and Joseph kept on going on the road that led away from their homeland.

4,5   Slowly, very slowly, they kept on going until the road came to Egypt.

2,3   Herod's soldiers would not go into Egypt.

1,4   Mary and Joseph stayed safely there until Herod was dead.

2,5   Then God told Joseph he could return to Israel once again.

3   They went back to Nazareth.

1,2   It had been a long time since they had been home.

Suggested Musical Interlude   "The First Noel"
                                       verses 1 and 2

4   Nothing important could come from Nazareth.

3,5   Nothing important could ever happen there.

1,2,3   Joseph was a carpenter and Mary was a dedicated wife and mother.

1,4,5   It was a very common place, Nazareth.

2,4,5   And Mary and Joseph were common, also.

1,3   They were just local people who had returned after a long absence.

1,5	They had with them a new child.
2,3,4	And he would live there, too.
ALL	His name was Jesus.
1	The son of a carpenter,
1,2	Immanuel,
3,4	The son of a woman named Mary.
ALL	Prince of Peace,
4	The Nazarene,
1,5	Almighty God,
2,3,4	A baby born in the Bethlehem countryside,
ALL	Eternal king,
3	Mighty counselor!
4,5	Savior!
2,3	Loving friend.
1,2	Alleluia!
3	Christ has come.
ALL	Merry Christmas!
5	Amen!

Suggested Music   "Joy To The World"
                                     verses 1 and 2

Scripture quotations are from the *New Revised Standard Version of the Bible* (NRSV), the *Revised Standard Version of the Bible* (RSV) and the *Holy Bible, New International Version* (NIV).

8

Let Every Heart Prepare Him Room

A Children's Christmas Play
By Suzanne Fisher

Speaking Parts
Large Mouse Named Moose
Friend Mouse Named Moe
Sister Mouse Named Marie
Donkey Named Fred/Joan (male or female)
Donkey Named Dawn
Rooster/Hen Named Rudy/Ruby (male or female)
Speckled Hen Named Fawn
Camel Named Claude
Camel Named Carrie
Lamb Named Leo
Lamb Named Lisa
Speaking Angel
Narrator

Nonspeaking Parts
Star Holder (or suspended)
Angels (if needed)
Mary
Joseph
Wise Man 1 — Frankincense
Wise Man 2 — Gold
Wise Man 3 — Myrrh
Shepherd Boys (if needed)

Other Personnel
Spotlight Controller
Costume Makers
Set Creators

Stable will need
Plastic for floor
Platform for Mary and Joseph
Stepladder for Angel

Bales of hay
Stepladder for Star Holder
   or suspended star

Simple costumes for
1 Narrator/s (dress up)
2 Donkeys
1 Speckled Hen
2 Lambs
1 Joseph
1 Star (or suspended star)
Angels and Lambs (as needed)

3 Mice
1 Rooster
2 Camels
1 Mary
3 Wise Men
1 Angel
Shepherd Boys (as needed)

If costumes are unavailable for animals, draw a picture of each animal on poster board. Tape a paper towel roll for a holder on back of picture. Children hold picture in front of them. For Mary, Joseph, Shepherds, and Wise Men, use bathrobes or extra large T-shirts with belts, ropes, or ties. Headgear can be towels tied with rope or ties.

Props needed
Podium for Narrator/s
One baby doll
Stable frame (optional)
Flowered hat for Marie
Gold (painted vase)
Myrrh (glass vase)

One crib
Large star with long point
Fake glasses for Moe
Two spotlights (white, blue)
Frankincense (glass vase)
Shepherd boys' staffs (tree
   limbs)

If children are too young to have speaking parts, Narrator/s can read entire play and choir can sing carols.

Let Every Heart Prepare Him Room

(Scene opens with white spotlight on NARRATOR. *All creatures in place in stable.)*

Narrator: A long time ago
in a faraway place,
there stood a little town
with very little space.

ALL *sing first verse*   "O Little Town Of Bethlehem"

Narrator: And in this little town,
there stood a stable stall.
It was the sheltered home
of creatures, great and small.

(Blue spotlight on stable)

Narrator: A big gray mouse named Moose
lived in a pile of hay,
tucked into one corner
safely out of the way.

Narrator: He had a mouse friend, Moe,
who was smart as could be,
and a small gray sister,
whose first name was Marie.

Narrator: They shared their hay-strewn home
with donkeys, Fred and Dawn,
a rooster they called Rudy
and a speckled hen named Fawn.

Narrator: The camels, Claude and Carrie,
Leo and Lisa lamb,
also found a home here
when not roaming the land.

Narrator:	Now Moose called out to Moe:
Moose:	Hey, Smarty, can you see
	that brightly shining star
	pointing down at you and me?

ALL *sing second verse*   "The First Noel"

Narrator:	Moe looked up in wonder,
	scratching his little chin.
Moe:	I know about this star,
Narrator:	He said.
	And he began to grin.

Narrator:	Then scampering Marie came
	to see the awesome sight.
	The donkeys brayed; the chickens clucked;
	they all were in a fright.

Moe:	Now calm down, everybody,
Narrator:	Moe shouted above the noise.
Moe:	This star will not harm us.
	It's a sign to rejoice.

Narrator:	Just then a man and lady
	came into the creatures' home.

(Enter MARY *and* JOSEPH. JOSEPH *helps* MARY *sit in hay.)*

	The man made a soft place
	for the lady to sit on.

Narrator:	The creatures grew quiet,
	not knowing how to act.
	Then Moose puffed up his big gray chest
	and started to react.

Narrator:	Moe pulled him back by the tail and told him to behave.
Moe:	These are very special people sent here to be safe.
Narrator:	Moose yanked his long tail free and glared at his good friend.
Moose:	Whatever do you mean? I do not want to lend my home and hay to strangers whatever you believe. Why are they so special? I'm gonna make them leave!
Marie:	No, please!
Narrator:	Pleaded Marie.
Rudy/Ruby:	Moe is right,
Narrator:	Said Rudy.
Narrator:	Nudging Big Moose, Dawn said:
Dawn:	Calm down, and you will see.
Narrator:	Carrie and Claude shushed them:
Carrie & Claude:	Be quiet, we hear a sound.
Narrator:	They all hushed and listened. Wide-eyed, they turned around.
Narrator:	In the lady's arms, lay a precious bundle, cooing and gurgling. The creatures were quite humbled.

ALL *sing first verse*   "Away In The Manger"

Narrator:	Inching closer, Moose took a peek and then he smiled wide. This was no usual man-child. He was filled with love inside.

ALL *sing first verse*   "What Child Is This?"

Narrator: Leo looked up and saw the star,
Leo: It points to the Babe.
Narrator: Lisa said at the Wise Men's approach,
(Enter WISE MEN*)*
Lisa: A long journey they have made.

ALL *sing first verse*   "We Three Kings"

Narrator: Reverently, they laid down gifts:
                       gold, frankincense and myrrh.
(Lay gifts in front of babe)
                       They bowed their heads in respect.
                       Not a single word was heard.

Narrator: Happy tears filled the creatures' eyes.
Fred/Joan: I heard the angels say:
Angels: This is God's Son, sent to you,
                       bringing love and joy today.

ALL *sing first verse*   "Hark! The Herald Angels Sing"

Narrator: They wiped away joyful tears.
Fawn: Look around for gifts to give.
Narrator: But all they had was their stable stall,
                       the home in which they lived.

(ALL pick up hay, approach cradle, kneel, and hold out hay to-wards cradle.)

Narrator: Joyfully, led by Moose,
                       they began to bring new hay
                       to make God's Son more comfortable,
                       welcoming his stay.

(Spotlight on NARRATOR*)*

Narrator: A long time ago,
far, far away,
even the creatures knew
what we know today.

That God, the Creator
of every living thing,
sent His Son to save our souls,
Jesus, King of kings.

Out of meager hay,
they prepared a place for Him.
Let us prepare room in our hearts
and welcome Jesus in.

ALL *sing first verse*   "Joy To The World"

Ask Congregation to join in singing next verses "Joy To The World"

Lights out